In memory of
Molly McArthur

*Late people
are still loved*

Contents

Foreword

When you invent a fictional character you give a hostage to fortune: the character does not belong just to you – he or she belongs to readers and to the world at large. So others may propose to give your character a larger life, whether on the screen or in some other context. Most authors are wary of this – and understandably so; many literary characters have been made to do and say things they would never dream of doing in the hands of their original begetter.

It was a happy day for me when Stuart Brown came to ask me if he could write a Mma Ramotswe cookbook. I already knew Stuart and I was confident that he would produce something with which I – and Mma Ramotswe – would be perfectly happy. I knew that he had made a very detailed study of the books and indeed it seemed to me that he knew more about them than I did myself. Authors often forget the details.

When Stuart showed me a draft of the book I was astonished at the extent to which food is mentioned in the original books. I do not remember endowing these books with quite so many culinary references, but there is no doubt that I did. That is not because Mma Ramotswe is a glutton – it is just that she often thinks about things when cooking or eating, and so it was understandable, then, that there should be a fair number of references to food.

The cuisine of sub-Saharan Africa is not widely known in the wider world. This book is to be welcomed in redressing that situation and in bringing to the attention of readers some of the tasty dishes with which the cooks of Africa – many of them women very much like Mma Ramotswe – feed their families. Do not look for great culinary elaboration here – look instead for good, nutritious fare, exactly the sort of food that we can imagine gracing the table as Mma Ramotswe sits down to dinner with Mr J.L.B. Matekoni and the children after a hard day's work in the No. 1 Ladies' Detective Agency and Tlokweng Road Speedy Motors. Can I smell pumpkin? I think I can. Do I hear the sound of cattle lowing in the distance? I think I do. Is all well in the kitchens of Botswana? I think it is.

Alexander McCall Smith

Letlhafula: harvest thanksgiving

Introduction

This book began with a meal. In 2001, I found myself sitting next to Alexander McCall Smith at a conference dinner in Stockholm. There was a great deal of laughter around the table and cooking was discussed, the concept of 'unreconstructed males' touched upon and the name Elizabeth David mentioned in exalted tones.

Upon joining the millions who appreciate Alexander McCall Smith's affectionate and humorous tales, I was struck by the prominence of cooking and eating in the stories. Sharing Mma Ramotswe's relish for food, I suggested a cookbook to McCall Smith who has been hugely encouraging throughout the process.

The result has no pretensions to being a definitive guide to the cookery of Botswana, but is written in a spirit of celebration for the people and the place. It seeks to offer a flavour of the foods dear to Mma Ramotswe as well as an approving appraisal of the traditional build, the larger-sized figure that signifies prosperity and the enlightened state of being at ease in one's own skin. The book also reproduces recipes from people in Botswana, keen to share their cuisine with others everywhere, because they are kind-hearted and love their country.

Whilst many of the ingredients required are to be found online and internationally in African grocers and butchers, some remain elusive outside Botswana. Where possible, alternatives are suggested and a glossary of terms is provided at the back as well as an index.

I hope that you will enjoy this book, whether as a companion to McCall Smith's stories; for the beautiful photography and design; as a stove-side recipe guide; or a gentle encouragement to explore Botswana.

Stuart Brown
August 2009

Chapter 1

Bush Tea Beginnings

Mma Ramotswe was always the first to rise in the morning, and she enjoyed the brief private time before the others would get up and start making demands of her. There would be breakfast to prepare, children's clothes to find, husband's clothes to find too; there would be a hundred things to do. But that lay half an hour or so ahead; for the time being she could be alone in her garden, as the sun came up over the border to the east, beyond Tlokweng, hovering over the horizon like a floating ball of fire. There was no finer time of day than this, she thought, when the air was cool and when, amidst the lower branches of the trees, there was still a hint, just the merest hint, of translucent white mist. (The Miracle at Speedy Motors)

Mma Ramotswe has a pot of redbush tea in Africa, at the foot of Kgale Hill. Each day dawns with a deep red brew and the familiar chorus of cattle bells on Radio Botswana, unchanged since Precious was a little girl waiting by the fire in Mochudi with her dear daddy, the late Obed Ramotswe, expert judge of cattle.

The first cup of tea is enjoyed sitting in peace on the veranda in Zebra Drive watching the birds, or whilst taking a stroll around the yard. Mma Ramotswe doesn't officially count the two cups that she enjoys during this, her favourite time of day, when no demands are being made of her as a wife, a mother and the proprietor of the No. 1 Ladies' Detective Agency.

Observing the old Botswana ways, tea must be offered to others before replenishing one's own cup and is regarded by Mma Ramotswe as a temporary solution in many cases, helping clients to talk, putting them at their ease and taking their minds off their fears for a moment. Mma Makutsi, *Associate* Detective, who had gained a peerless ninety-seven per cent at the Botswana Secretarial College, was clear in her own mind that she drank a good deal less tea than her employer's six cups a day, a figure that did not include top-ups.

Rooibos

Redbush tea is also known in Botswana as *Rooibos*, literally, 'red bush' in Afrikaans, and *Radikgonnyana* in Setswana, meaning 'small sticks'. The tea comes from the *rooibos* shrub (*Aspalathus linearis*) in the Western Cape of South Africa, the needle-like leaves of which turn red when fermented and dried in the sun. *Rooibos* is naturally caffeine free and doesn't induce the slight fluttering of the heart for Mma Ramotswe that coffee and China tea set off. In the past, in many villages in Botswana, it was common to add milk to the pot as soon as the boiling water was poured in and for the pot to be placed on the hot coals for the tea leaves and liquids to work their magic. The Redbush Tea Company[1] gives a percentage of its profits to the Kalahari Peoples Fund (KPF)[2].

Whereas in some countries during World War II, sugar rations went into cakes, in Botswana sugar continued to go into tea. Many people in Botswana do have a sweet tooth when it comes to their drinks and today it is acceptable to add condensed milk to tea (as Mma Makutsi has been known to do), or honey, cow's milk, a sprig of fresh Botswana mint or of 'Resurrection Bush' which make a delicious addition to a brew. This resourceful herb is so-called because once picked, it can be stored in a favourite tin for many months and when plunged into water, bright green leaves will miraculously burst open. A sprig of this added to the bath is also said to have the power to enhance male potency.

1   www.redbushtea.com
2   www.kalaharipeoples.org

There is a good deal more to be said on the important subject of tea, but tea is surely much better with a biscuit.

Biscuits

Her Saturdays were something of a ritual. She always went to the President Hotel for tea in the morning, and then, after a quick shopping trip, she would return and make lunch. In the afternoon she would have a nap, as Mr J.L.B. Matekoni also sometimes did, before getting up to make biscuits for tea. (Tea Time for the Traditionally Built)

The scale of Mma Ramotswe's biscuit output is very much more modest than that of Prince Charles, of whom Mma Ramotswe has read. She had determined that one or two of the plain Marie biscuits would definitely make space in the tin labelled 'pencils' if ever a royal biscuit should happen along. After all, these were biscuits not only of a royal, but of a man who respects cattle.

Lemon and Condensed Milk Biscuits

Makes around 24 2-inch diameter biscuits

These egg-free biscuits are light, yet rich. Friends or family should appreciate the traditionally built lady rousing herself from a well deserved rest and, as she fills the home with the warm smell of baking, such a provider may wish to check that condensed milk, spooned straight from the tin, tastes quite as delicious as she remembers it. Members of the community look to 'ladies with a reputation for baking' to answer such questions and it is important not to disappoint.

Ingredients:

12 oz plain flour	8 oz unsalted butter
2 tsp baking powder	½ tsp lemon juice
½ tsp grated lemon rind	4 oz caster sugar
7 fl. oz condensed milk	Small quantity icing sugar
Pinch of salt	

Method:

Cream butter and sugar well.

Add condensed milk and beat until well mixed.

Sift flour, baking powder, salt and add to the butter mixture, with lemon juice and grated rind.

Beat until thoroughly mixed through.

Grease two large baking trays, or line with greaseproof paper.

Take teaspoons of the mix and roll gently into 1 inch balls and place on baking tray.

Flatten gently with a fork until they are about ¼ inch thick and ensure they have room for manoeuvre to avoid sticking together.

Bake at 170°C for 12 – 15 minutes (160°C fan-assisted oven).

Cool on the tray.

Dust very lightly with icing sugar.

Mealie Meal Biscuits

Makes about 40

Ingredients:

1½ cups of flour	½ cup fine mealie meal
½ cup dried coconut	6 tbs shortening (butter, margarine)
¾ cup white sugar	1 tsp baking powder
1 egg	Small pinch salt
2 tsp milk	A few currants or sultanas

Method:

Sieve the flour, mealie meal, salt and baking powder and mix together. Rub in the shortening very finely, until the mixture is like fine breadcrumbs. Add the sugar and coconut and mix well all together. Beat the egg and mix with the milk. Stir this into the dry mixture, adding a very little milk if required to make a firm dough. Roll out the dough on a floured table, or board, and cut into little biscuits with a cutter or a small glass. Put the biscuits on a lightly greased baking tray and press a currant or sultana on top of each biscuit. Bake the biscuits in a moderate hot oven, 200°C for about 10 minutes until lightly browned and cooked.

Bambara Groundnut *(Setswana, manoko a be sitsweng)*

Grown in Botswana, these larger than average peanuts or 'monkeynuts' are very tasty and enjoyed as a snack. The nutritious nuts can be boiled or roasted in their shells, seasoned with chilli, or pepper and salt and eaten shelled. They can be eaten fresh, or sun-dried. They are also a staple ingredient in some traditional dishes.

Groundnut Biscuits

Makes about 48

Ingredients:

½ cup margarine	½ cup peanut butter
½ cup groundnuts	2 cups sifted flour
½ tsp salt	1 cup sugar
2 eggs, well beaten	¼ cup milk
2 tsp baking powder	

Method:

Heat oven to 190°C. Grease a large baking sheet. Chop the groundnuts, but do not make the pieces too small. Cream the margarine until it is light. Slowly add the sugar and peanut butter, and cream together until fluffy. Mix in beaten egg and milk. Sift together flour, baking powder and salt. Stir into the first mixture, making a very stiff dough. Then add chopped nuts. Use a teaspoon to put small pieces of dough on to the baking sheet. Leave space for them to spread. Bake for 15 minutes or until nicely brown.

Pragmatism and Loose Purists

A pragmatist, Mma Ramotswe has succumbed to the use of teabags. As a romantic, a patriot and staunch defender of the old Botswana ways, she also continues to use loose tea, on occasions, enjoying the frisson of getting the odd tea leaf in her mouth. At home in Extension Two, Grace Makutsi uses her old round tea caddy showing Botswana's former administrative capital, Mafeking, also once a regular shopping haunt of Mma Ramotswe's prior to the growth of Gaborone which today sells anything one might want. Mma Makutsi follows the time-honoured recipe of 'one spoon for each mouth and one for the pot' and knows that her employer likes her tea fresh from the pot, piping hot.

She loved standing in the kitchen, stirring the pot, thinking over the events of the day, sipping at a large mug of bush tea which she balanced on the edge of the stove. (The No. 1 Ladies' Detective Agency)

Tea is the essential 'cook's tipple' and Mma Ramotswe invariably has her favourite brown patterned teapot from the Gabane Pottery, within easy reach of the stove. She saves her special commemorative Queen Elizabeth II tea cup for use at meal-times and enjoys the edgy *je ne sais quoi* that the greasy finger marks on the mugs at Tlokweng Road Speedy Motors bring to the already distinctive taste. Tea drinkers should insist that their pots are treated with respect. Fresh in Mma Ramotswe's mind is the calamitous incident where the older Apprentice, Charlie, had used Mma Makutsi's new china teapot as a receptacle for engine oil. This had unleashed a catalogue of events including Charlie calling Mma Makutsi a warthog and storming off.

Happiest when travelling into the Bush, Mma Ramotswe has the foresight to plan possible bush tea stops along the way, but always makes the provision of travelling with a supply of teabags. While the motto of the Botswana Secretarial College is 'Be Acurate', Mma Ramotswe favours 'Be Prepared' and carrying bush tea is a totem of preparedness. In a bid to avoid running out of teabags, Rra Polopetsi had been put in charge of stock control, his having volunteered the need for a system, drawing upon his knowledge from the pharmacy. Whilst defused by Mma Ramotswe's smile and a knowing look between the two ladies, this  unbidden suggestion of introducing new practices has been accurately chronicled as: 'a moment of electric tension, thrilling in retrospect . . . dangerous to a degree'. On the matter of tea for the detective on the move, it must be understood that coffee is an entirely different drink and that the serving of tea from a coffee flask leaves an unpleasant taste in the mouth for some time, but not quite as long as such transgressions linger in the minds of those victim to tainted *Rooibos*.

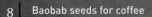
| Baobab seeds for coffee

Baobab

The trunk of the mighty Baobab (*Mowana* in Setswana) is of a remarkably traditional build, its circumference ranging from 15 to an incredible 150 feet. These astonishingly capacious trees have been used variously as a house, bar, shop and even prison. The Baobab is known as the 'upside down tree' because its slender branches reaching into the African sky, resemble roots. The lore of the Bushmen has it that the god Thora rejected it from his garden and threw it out of Paradise and that this explains why one seems to encounter only mature Baobab trees. Their saplings are regarded as difficult to recognise as they have such different leaves from the mature specimens.

Longevity is another remarkable characteristic of the Baobab, some living to the age of 3,000 years. As their age testifies, Baobabs are extremely hardy, but when their time is up, they rot from the inside and fall to a fibrous heap, giving rise to the belief that this magical tree doesn't die, but vanishes.

Superstition has it that if you pick one of the snow-white flowers of the Baobab that come out at night, you will be eaten by a lion, a danger to which Mma Ramotswe is ever alert.

As well as creating homes for many creatures in the Bush, these unmissable ancients produce pods that can be up to a foot long. Their hard husks are pale grey-green with a velvety texture on the outside and contain a sweet white pulp that tastes of cream of tartar. Each pod houses dozens of large seeds which are covered by a whitish, powdery substance as well as stringy matter (which you don't eat). Baobab provides six times more Vitamin C than an orange and twice as much calcium as milk. It supplies snacks in the form of the seeds (which are tart but delicious when sucked, or they can be roasted) and the flesh is eaten fresh or dried. According to legend, if you drink water in which the seeds of the Baobab have been soaked, you will be protected against crocodile attack – now there's a 'health drink'.

Baobab Tree Coffee

The seeds of the Baobab are the source of a perfectly serviceable coffee, ideal for emergencies in the Bush if one has run out of sachets of redbush tea:

Ingredients:
A Baobab pod
Sugar, to taste

Method:
Dissolve the white substance until the brown seeds remain.
Allow seeds to dry.
Crush seeds into a fine powder with a mortar and pestle.
Separate the powder from the grains.
Use powder as you would coffee, adding boiled water and as many sugars as you like.

Baobab Lemonade

This drink involves no more than making a hole in the Baobab pod the night before you want to drink and filling it with water. Add sugar or honey to taste, since it will be quite tart.

Termite mounds were sometimes used as ovens

10

Motlopi

The evergreen *Motlopi* is also known as the 'Shepherd's Tree' or 'Tree of Life', as it is appreciated by both animals and humans. *Motlopi* roots can be turned into *Kota*, a form of sugar and are also used in a preparation to treat haemorrhoids. Its fruit is fermented to make a drink called *Khuki* and its flower buds are a substitute for capers in pickling. Superstition has it that if the *Motlopi* fruits wither before the millet crop is ripe, the harvest will fail and if the wood of the tree (commonly used to produce utensils) is burnt, cows will produce only bull calves. An infusion made with *Motlopi* leaves is a traditional cure for eye infections in cattle.

The roots of the *Motlopi* tree are also used in some villages to make a traditional coffee substitute which aids digestion and provides some income for people in rural areas. A million miles away from 'instant', its production is arduous, involving digging for deep-set roots which need to be split, shredded and stored overnight to begin fermentation. They are then dried in the sun, fried in vegetable oil until they turn golden brown and pounded into a powder. The resulting drink can be quite strong and bitter but may stave off the withdrawal symptoms of the coffee drinker.

Motlopi Root Coffee

Method:

Dig out some *Motlopi* roots. The roots must have a sweet taste. It is said that the *Motlopi* tree with the sweetest roots is the one that grows nearest to a termite mound. Crush the roots with a mortar and pestle, dry in the sun and store. When dry, cook until brown without anything added to it, and pound again. Store in an airtight container. Use two or three spoonfuls of the coffee, boiling it with water for 5 minutes.

Ginger Beer (Gemere)

Perfect for picnics and parties, ginger beer is a favourite drink and Bishop Mwamba shared his family recipe with Mma Ramotswe.

Makes 9 pints

Ingredients:

**20 cups cold or boiled water
½ cup sugar
2 tbs ground ginger
3 tsp tartaric acid
3 tsp cream of tartar
1 cup raisins (optional)**

Method:

Pour water into a large container. Add sugar. Stir to dissolve.

Add the ginger and remaining ingredients.

Cover and keep in a warm place for 2 days to mature.

Sieve.

Chill before serving.

Persuasive fruitcake (see page

Is Green the 'New Red'?

Mma Makutsi has had a troubled, off-and-on relationship with bush tea, trying hard to like it so as not to upset Mma Ramotswe, but having been unable to contain the truth, confessing that her heart lies with the non-bush, China variety. This revelation came as a thunderbolt to Mma Ramotswe and threw her into soul-searching about the rights and wrongs of offering a choice of tea to others. Unbeknown to Mma Makutsi, her fiancé, Phuti Radiphuti, Manager of the Double Comfort Furniture Store actually prefers redbush to China tea, but has not quite found the right moment to broach the subject with his betrothed.

Mosukudu **Tea and** *Mosukujane* **(Wild Mint Tea)**

Abundant in Botswana, *Mosukudu* is a wild mint which when made into tea, smells and tastes of a pleasant, but not overpowering nor toothpaste-like mint. Its leaves are broader and thicker than those of the other variety of mint that grows wild, *Mosukujane*, which is lighter and sweeter. As with *Rooibos*, these mint infusions are naturally caffeine free and are said to be good for cleansing the system.

An old friend of Mma Ramotswe's, Mma Glickman, who is helping to keep the old Botswana ways alive, teaching school groups and visitors out at Bahurutse Cultural Lodge had rekindled Mma Ramotswe's interest in *Mosukudu* bush tea. As so many traditional things came back into fashion, Mma Makutsi wondered whether *Mosukudu* might become the new tea *du jour* of her employer. In shoes, Mma Makutsi knew, it was important to keep up with this season's colour. Might *green* bush tea become 'the new red' and remove a little of the tension that exists between the poles of redbush and China? Mma Makutsi made a note in her 'Incidental and Interim Reports' file to investigate this exciting possibility.

Making Time for Cake

Cake, of course, goes so terribly well with tea and has a universality that straddles the bush/China divide. Even for one who appreciates that cooking the evening meal takes time, there have to be sacrifices and cake-making is one such casualty that Mma Ramotswe has been working to resuscitate. The indomitable Matron of the Orphan Farm, Mma Potokwani said that one had to *make* time.

Mma Potokwani knew very well the fondness that Mma Ramotswe and Mr J.L.B. Matekoni both had for the Orphan Farm fruitcake; there was a deep, silent rapture to it which she fully understood. The Senior girls made this cake entirely proficiently and to Mma Ramotswe's satisfaction, but whenever the Matron was expecting visitors, she enlisted the expertise of one of the House Mothers, Mma Gotofede, who shared her recipe with Mma Ramotswe. Some ladies are said to have hands for making pastry, others the touch for meringues and Mma Gotofede was recognised as an alchemist in producing her golden fruitcake.

Persuasive Fruitcake

Ingredients:

9 oz dried mixed fruit	4 oz chopped almonds
9 oz soft butter or margarine	7 oz caster sugar
4 eggs	11 oz flour
4 oz corn flour	3 tsp baking powder
Grated rind of 1 lemon	Icing sugar

Method:

Grease a 10-inch baking tin with some butter.

Preheat oven to 180°C – fan-assisted oven to 160°C.

Cream butter or margarine in mixer and add sugar.

Add eggs one at a time, mixing in thoroughly before adding the next egg, and continue until all the sugar has dissolved.

Sift flour, corn flour and baking powder over the butter mixture.

Once the flour mixture has been incorporated, add fruit mix, almonds and lemon rind.

Pour batter into baking tin and smooth over the top.

Bake cake for 1 hour and 15 minutes.

Remove from tin and cool on a rack.

Before serving, cover cake with sifted icing sugar.

Cake and the Art of Pump Maintenance

Mr J.L.B. Matekoni saw the cake, and for a moment he frowned. He knew Mma Potokwani, and the presence of a large cake, specially made for the occasion, was an unambiguous signal that she had a request to make of him. A cake of this size, and emitting such a strong smell of raisins, would mean a major mechanical problem.

(The Full Cupboard of Life)

The famous Orphan Farm pump

Mma Potokwani was herself an old hand at baking and stirred with the same vigour with which she changed gear and generally met life head-on. As far as Mma Ramotswe knew, the Matron followed the same recipe as Mma Gotofede (but the withholding of a magic ingredient or two was not unknown in the most competitive of cake- and jam-making circles) and her cake was spell-binding. Both Mma Ramotswe and Mr J.L.B. Matekoni knew that the formula for the cake's richness and the size of piece (or pieces) that slid hypnotically onto their plates, bore a direct correlation to the scale of the favour that would follow, yet each was rendered powerless in its presence.

'Cake,' said Mma Ramotswe quickly. 'That is Mr J.L.B. Matekoni's great weakness. He cannot help himself when it comes to cake. He can be manipulated very easily if he has a plate of cake in his hand.'

Mma Makutsi laughed. 'Mma Potokwani knows that, doesn't she?' she said. 'I have seen her getting Mr J.L.B. Matekoni to do all sorts of things for her just by offering him pieces of that fruitcake of hers.'

(Blue Shoes and Happiness)

While she instilled a proper African strictness and sense of Botswana values in the Orphan Farm, Mma Potokwani would do anything for the children entrusted to her care. A formidable advocate for them, she does not take 'no' for an answer from anyone who can provide support. In one such instance, the persuasive Matron, unleashing fruitcake upon an unsuspecting surgeon, had secured an operation on a child's leg. For Mr J.L.B. Matekoni, the invitation to visit Mma Potokwani and the subsequent sight of cake was a sure sign that the Orphan Farm pump, which should long since have been retired, needed his mechanical skills.

That was her technique, he now understood; just as Eve had used an apple to trap Adam, so Mma Potokwani used fruitcake. Fruitcake, apples; it made no difference really. Oh foolish, weak men!

(The Full Cupboard of Life)

Motholeli's Disappearing Banana Cake

Motholeli has found that her younger brother Puso can polish off her cake in just two days.

Ingredients:

3 bananas (quite ripe ones work best, although any bananas will do)
2 eggs
6 oz caster sugar
8 oz plain flour
1 tsp salt
1 tsp bicarbonate of soda
Demerara sugar (to sprinkle on top)

Method:

Squish the bananas in a bowl and mix in the beaten eggs. Add the caster sugar, flour, salt and bicarbonate of soda (no need to beat the mixture, just stir it well). Pour into a buttered loaf tin and sprinkle the top with the Demerara sugar. Bake in the oven at 160°C for 1 hour (best to check it after 50 minutes by putting a skewer in to test if it comes out clean – although check a few places as if you hit a lump of banana it won't come out clean). Leave it in the tin for a minute or two, and then turn out on to a cooling rack. Best eaten warm, spread with butter.

Mma Sechele's Ginger Date Loaf

This loaf comes out beautifully.

Ingredients:

1 lb dates
2 oz bicarbonate of soda
1 tsp mixed spice
4 cups plain flour or cake flour
1½ cups sugar
2 cups boiling water

5 oz butter
2 tsp cinnamon
2 tsp ground ginger
1 cup seedless raisins
2 eggs

Method:

Take a large bowl and add cut-up dates to the raisins. Add butter, eggs, sugar, bicarbonate of soda and spices. Pour boiling water over. Fold in and allow to cool. Fold in the flour.
Bake in two bread tins at 175°C for 1 hour.

The Traditional Build and Threats from Outside

She enjoyed her food, certainly, but she was also very active . . . All women had been that build, and it had brought them good fortune and success; there was no point, she felt, being a thin and unhappy person when the attractions of being a comfortable person were so evident. And men liked women like that too. It was a terrible thing that the outside world had done to Africa, bringing in the idea that slender ladies, some of them as thin as a sebokolodi, a millipede, should be considered desirable. That was not what men really wanted. Men wanted women whose shape reminded them of good things on the table.

(The Full Cupboard of Life)

The 'traditional build' is a stature that perhaps requires no explanation but which Mma Ramotswe, who buys size 22 blouses, once helpfully defined as: ' . . . the shape that African ladies are traditionally meant to be' (*Blue Shoes and Happiness*). Being well built equates to wellbeing and prosperity, a symbol of success and status. Prior to getting married, Mma Ramotswe had looked forward to feeding her husband up so that he would quickly put on weight and, as she put it 'look more like the prosperous garage owner he was'. Feeding your man properly is a sign of love, this proud form proving that a husband is being looked after and a well-built wife demonstrating that he, in turn, is being a good provider.

In Africa, well-built ladies have always been appreciated. Whilst unfocused on their work, one thing for which the two Apprentices could be relied upon was a frank appraisal of the appearance of women and representative of their countrymen, they would attest to the importance of the large, traditionally built bottom. Mma Ramotswe felt a little uncomfortable bringing to mind the predilections of these immature men but, like a compliment from a child, such an unfiltered testimonial made a compelling case for the statelier seat which had to be more comfortable than a bony bottom.

Mma Ramotswe was not an admirer of form achieved through avarice or ill-gotten gains. She recalled the spare parts man, Harry Moloso, with his beer belly (ample in its spareness), and Mma Tsau's greedy husband, whose stomach was so large from eating the best cuts of meat stolen from the catering college, that he could no longer see beyond his gut.

That would serve him right, thought Mma Ramotswe. Being a traditionally built lady was one thing; being a traditionally built man was quite another. And it was certainly not so good.

(The Full Cupboard of Life)

Importantly, to Mma Ramotswe, the larger frame signifies that a person shares her appreciation of the good things on their plate, values the opportunities they have, and makes the most of life, in all its abundance. Such a carriage bestowed an appropriate physical presence for commanding figures such as Mma Potokwani who had achieved, in Mma Ramotswe's eyes 'an unusually traditional shape'.

Mma Ramotswe was well aware of the difficulties now faced by traditionally built people, particularly by traditionally built ladies. There was a time in Botswana when nobody paid much attention to thin people – indeed thin people might sometimes simply not be seen at all, as they could so easily be looked past. If a thin person stood against a background of acacia trees and grass, then might he not either merge into the background or be thought to be a stick or even a shadow? This was never a danger with a traditionally built person; such a person would stand in the landscape with the same prominence and authority as a baobab tree.

(In the Company of Cheerful Ladies)

Mma Ramotswe strongly opposes, as quite wrong, the shape of self-neglect and starvation with which women in particular are force-fed by so-called 'fashion' and that dreadful thing 'consumerism'. She has no ambitions to resemble the 'terrible stick-thin creatures one saw in the advertisements' (*The No.1 Ladies' Detective Agency*). She would occasionally drift into reveries in which traditionally built ladies advertised dishes or ingredients and could imagine one day, the need for traditionally built ladies to make a stand against the new 'gym-and-cucumber-build' and this notion of 'lifestyle'. No, insidious attempts to dictate a woman's shape must be opposed and the traditionally built would represent a formidable force. 'Choose to eat what you want' is Mma Ramotswe's maxim, but make it a choice, rather than an escape or self-punishment and make it part of your own nourishing landscape.

She had a taste for sugar, however, and this meant that a doughnut or a cake might follow the sandwich. She was a traditionally built lady, after all, and she did not have to worry about dress size, unlike those poor neurotic people who were always looking in mirrors and thinking that they were too big. What was too big anyway? Who was to tell another person what size they should be? It was a form of dictatorship, by the thin, and she was not having any of it. If these thin people became any more insistent, then the more generously-sized people would just have to sit on them! Hah!

(Morality for Beautiful Girls)

Honeymooners: flying termites are gathered at night

Healthier Snacks

Small boys knew . . . the best place to find flying ants when the rains caused the termites to crawl up from their subterranean burrows and rise up into the sky, unless a small boy snatched them first, tore off their fluttering wings, and popped them, delicious morsels, into his mouth . . .

(Tea Time for the Traditionally Built)

Roasted Flying Ants (*Setswana Dintlhwa*)

These flying ants swarm in huge clouds during the rains in November to December and local people in Botswana know when conditions are right for their arrival. The termites are collected at night and the wings removed. They are gently pan fried with a little butter or oil and salt. Once allowed to cool, they are enjoyed as a sweet, buttery snack that tastes not unlike salted peanuts. They can be dried and stored, without refrigeration, for several months. They taste sandy, but are high in protein and are sometimes pounded into a powder by the San bushmen, providing a high-protein addition to meals over a number of months.

Dried Mopane Worms

High in protein but also very seasonal, they are only available for a few months a year, normally towards the end of summer. They are actually caterpillars which are harvested from particular trees *(see p.93)*.

Boiled Phane (*Mopane Worms*)

Wash 2 cups of dried *phane* (*Mopane* worms) and place in a pot with 1½ cups of water. Cook for 15 minutes and then add 1½ tablespoons of oil. Cook the *phane* until soft and season with salt and pepper.

Chicken Feet and Chicken Livers, considered a real treat snack.

Letshotlho (fresh cooked dried mealies)

The kernels of a green (unripe) maize cob or 'mealie' is parboiled and then dried. They retain their bite and are tasty eaten with a refreshing drink.

Dried Melon Slices (*Lengangale*) and also their seeds, roasted (too many cause constipation).

Butternut or Pumpkin Seeds Salted and baked or grilled.

Wild Truffles (*Mahupu*) The Kalahari desert truffle is eaten boiled and salted.

Biltong (*Setswana, Segwapa*) Dried beef, or game meat, similar to American beef jerky *(see p.101)*.

Morula Stix Strips of dried morula fruit pulp, harvested and manufactured in Botswana by WildFoods, whose work supports local communities and who also produce morula jam and jelly and tasty chocolate clusters containing morula nut.

More Wild Fruits

Mogorogorwane *(Strichnos cocculoides)*
Eaten fresh, is the size and shape of an orange, with a hard shell and brown, jelly-like flesh. Has large seeds with a very low strychnine content. The fruit is often picked green, before the baboons get them and then buried in the ground for several weeks to ripen.

Morojwa *(Azanza garckeana)*
Hard, thick-skinned, segmented fruit. The hard, thick skins are chewed. A sweet slime eventually separates from the fibre. The inside is dry with seeds. Commonly known as chewing gum or snot apple!

Mmilo *(Vangueria infausta)*
Popular, plum-sized fruit with thin skin and pasty flesh which tastes just like stewed apple.
Eaten fresh or made into a tasty cool drink by adding sugar and water.

Moretlwa *(Grewia flava)*
Little berry with large seed. Flesh dries with high sugar content. Eaten fresh or dried and stored as raisins. Makes such a potent alcoholic drink that its production is banned by many chiefs.

Mupudu *(Mimusops zeyheri)*
Small yellow/orange fruit with dry, pasty flesh. Very pleasant to eat when ripe. One or two medium-sized pips. Seeds are pounded, pips removed and then shaped into small cakes. Stores well.

Mohawa *(Ficus abutilifolia)*
Lots of small, hard figs grow along the stems which are often insect-infested. Eaten fresh or made into jam.

Moretologa *(Ximenia caffra; X. americana)*
Yellow to red elongated fruit, thumb-sized or smaller. Large, oil-bearing seed. It can be very refreshing to suck the flesh when thirsty and particularly welcome when wandering in the bush. Skin highly astringent. Makes good jam.

Mopipi *(Boschia foetida)*
Similar fruit to Motlopi, but not so pleasant. Fruit eaten fresh.

Mogose *(Bauhinia petersiana)*
Tree bean pods are dried and beans stored. Beans are roasted for coffee. Widely used in the past.

Mosilabele *(Rhus lancea)*
Small dry fruit. Also used in making mead.

Mopenweeng *(Pappea capensis)*
Small cherry-like red fruit in capsule which opens when ripe. Sweet/sour taste. Eaten fresh or made into jam. Believed to be high in Vitamin C. Seeds contain edible oil.

nuts and seeds are popular snacks

More Wild Fruits

Motsotsojane *(Grewia flavescens)*
Small dry berry with large seed. The fibrous flesh is chewed and seed spat out. Refreshing to eat when walking on hot day in the bush. Soak for 28 hours and strain for a refreshing drink.

Mokopakopa *(Bridelia mollis)*
Round black berries. Eaten fresh or made into jam.

Herbaceous Plants

Morama *(Tylosema esculenta)*
Large bean size of a fat broad bean with a hard shell. Same nutritional content as soya. Roasted as snack. Can also be eaten as an accompaniment. Perennial tuber (delicious when young) grows to over 100 years old. Found in the Kalahari desert.

Leruswa *(Fockea angustifolea)*
Large tuber with watery, milky juice. Eaten and good source of moisture. Grows in Kalahari desert.

Kgopo *(Cyanotis speciosa)*
Edible tuber/rhizome. Roasted in hot ash.

Segwete
Thick tapering root. Eaten raw.

Mosisa *(Pygmaeothamnus zeyheri)*
Large, tasty yellowish fruits. Fruits very tasty. Low plants that grow in sandy areas.

Bokwidi
Bulbous root is edible.

Legabala *(Coccinea sessilifolia)*
Red and whitish elongated fruit on a creeper. Eaten both raw and cooked.

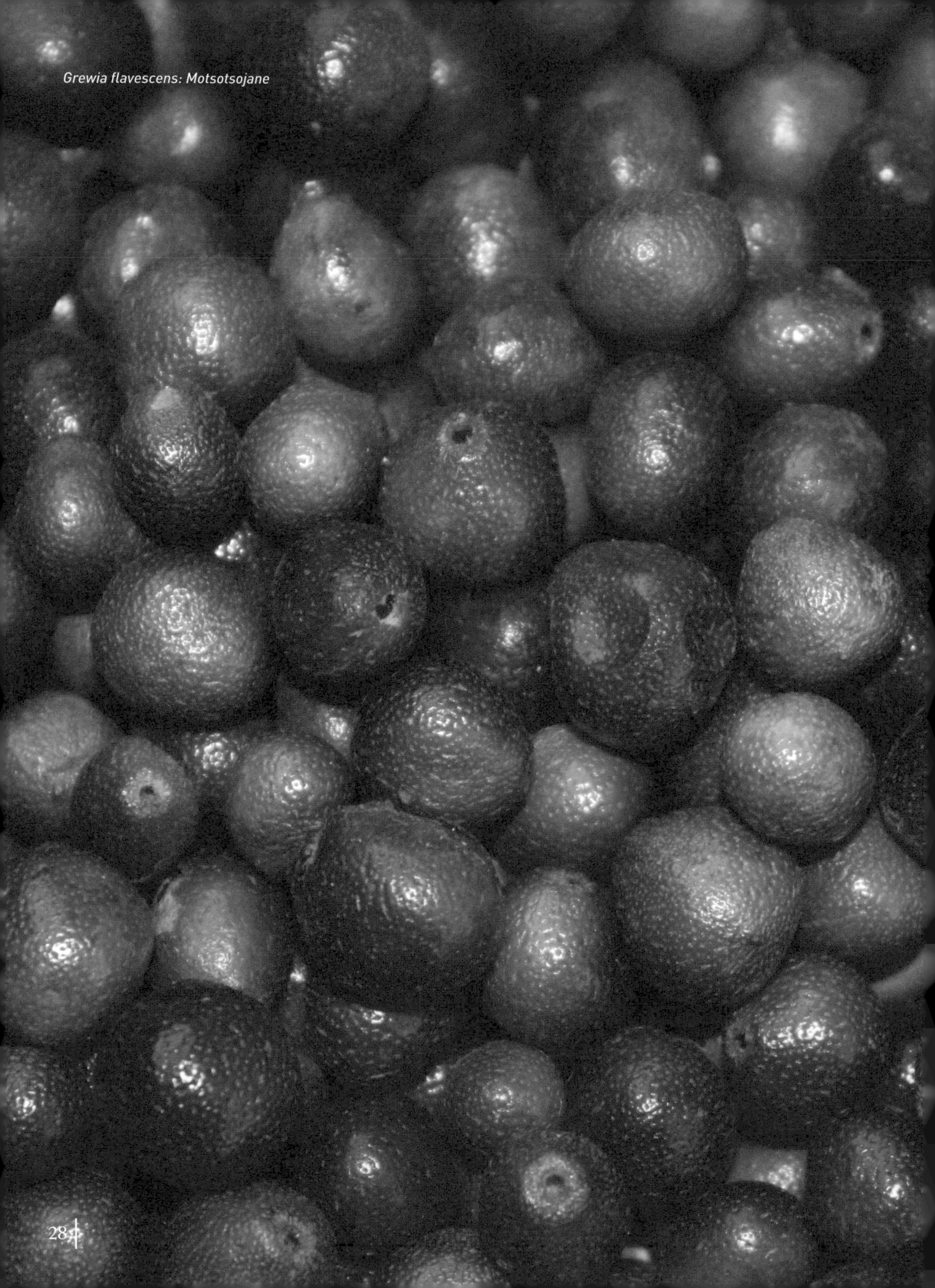

Grewia flavescens: Motsotsojane

'A balanced diet,' he said wisely. 'They say a balanced diet is the key to health.' There was silence for a moment as they reflected on his observation.
(Tears of the Giraffe)

Mma Ramotswe is clear in her personal conviction as to the importance of appreciating real food, freshly prepared, and she eats well, enjoying nutritious meals, the delicious fruit and protein-rich snacks of Botswana along with its sweeter treats. Like many of her brothers and sisters who have the opportunity, she eats with gusto but not often unconsciously. Nowadays Mma Ramotswe only has a cooked lunch at weekends or makes do with a snack or a glass of milk, but this is balanced by a cake or doughnut. Choice, in Mma Ramotswe's book, is a great luxury and one that she exercises, consciously.

Fruit and Vegetables

In common with their brothers and sisters throughout Africa, many Batswana have a passion for the delicious fruit in their country, regarding it with the same sort of excitement that others have for chocolate or cream-cake treats. Botswana offers both variety and quality. Anyone who has eaten an orange plucked straight from the tree or been handed the juice of freshly squeezed persimmon, pineapple, guava or mango will know that these resemble a different species – think the Berlin Philharmonic as opposed to 'the Really Terrible Orchestra'.

Although most are not native to Botswana and a good deal is imported, an array of choice is available in Southern Africa. Sorghum, millet, pumpkin, squash, mealies (maize) and melon are widespread. The following are cultivated on small farms and vegetable plots such as that of Mr J.L.B. Matekoni: green and runner beans, carrots, tomatoes, peppers, cabbage, onion, potatoes and sweet potato, cassava, beetroot, lettuce and Swiss chard, to name but a few.

A typical fruit salad is given a huge burst of flavour if you include passion fruit. Or perhaps try avocado as a dessert, with lemon and caster sugar. *Morogo* is the Setswana term for dark green, leafy vegetables which include wild spinach, *Rothwe* and *Thepe*. *Rothwe* is more bitter, and slightly tougher. These greens are often used to make a relish *(see p.96)*, which is served with sorghum meal or mealie meal *(see p.39)*.

Constipation – a 'Constitutional' Issue

Now constipation was quite a different matter. It would be dreadful for the whole world to know about troubles of that nature. She felt terribly sorry for people who suffered from constipation, and she knew there were many who did. There were probably enough of them to form a political party – with a chance of government perhaps . . . (The No. 1 Ladies' Detective Agency)

In Botswana many people are aware of the nutritional benefits of foods they eat and discuss with ease the effect that too much or too little of a particular foodstuff will have on the system. Porridge is high in fibre, which is good for one's constitution, as are bitter aloes, but porridge tastes so much better.

Mma Ramotswe understands that there are very grave illnesses associated with eating which require the same professional treatment, care and love to overcome as any other disease, and that vulnerable people can need help in getting the nourishment they need. She had weaned Puso onto healthier foods and knew from a friend in the Ministry of Health that obesity in pre-school children had become a serious problem in Botswana, as elsewhere in the world. If allowed, the children in the Orphan Farm would have nothing but cake, when they need beans and onions and, if left unsupported, the 'bad girls' in the House of Hope were prone to take nothing but alcohol. There, Mr Bobologo ensures that self-care is encouraged, with restorative stews filling this temporary sanctuary with homely aromas.

Mma Ramotswe is alert to avoiding a hungry lion
ready for a traditionally built snack and
would not miss such a clear paw print

Wealth and the Importance of Rain

. . . none of them was malnourished as happened in so many other African countries. Botswana was a well-blessed country. Nobody starved and nobody languished in prison for his or her political beliefs . . . the Batswana could hold their heads up anywhere – anywhere.
(Tears of the Giraffe)

Mma Ramotswe often counted the blessings of her country, not least for its stability and good sense which was thanks to the wisdom and foresight of Sir Seretse Khama and his successors and to the good hearts of ordinary Batswana. There are poor people in Botswana, but the nation's ability to feed its people should be a matter of pride. Mma Ramotswe had read that a billion people in the world live on a dollar a day. Unsure how many zeros this totalled, she knew that the inhuman statistic amounted to far too many individuals, families and communities who had fire in their bellies but little to put in them.

Pula

Botswana is a dry country dominated by the Kalahari. Such is the importance of water that 'Pula' is both the denomination of Botswana's currency and the Setswana word for 'rain'. Botswana's national coat of arms bears the words 'Pula' and where 'Best Wishes' might be written at the end of a letter, the sentiment is expressed in this word.

Good rains meant full stomachs; drought meant thin cattle and wilted crops. (Morality for Beautiful Girls)

Botswana is a nation of farmers, skilled in coaxing crops out of the umber soils, where water is so precious, and in raising some of the finest cattle in the world. Mma Ramotswe's prayer is always the same and includes the wish for 'rain that would make the crops grow and the cattle fat . . .' (*The No. 1 Ladies' Detective Agency*). Mr J.L.B. Matekoni's assiduous duty to the water pump is driven by his knowledge that the Orphan Farm relies upon the vegetables it grows to eat.

Despite the availability of this hard-won natural produce, too many people are being seduced by ready-meals and the allure of foreign fast-food chains. Part of the march of internationalisation and the faster pace of career-driven living that is advancing across the country, fast food is mistakenly associated with prestige. Though Mma Ramotswe herself has a deep love of cattle, as did her father before her, she knows that keeping livestock which are the only asset for the survival of millions in Africa today, is a hard way of existing. Some, who are not constrained by life-threatening poverty and the strictures of circumstance, have other ideas about making their way in the world. Botswana's young people are as talented and able as anyone anywhere. She just hoped that they would not trade an oral tradition under the stars and family meals with laughter, intimacy and a sense of belonging for the promise of promotion, reality-TV dinners and the ping of a microwave.

Leteisi: German-print dresses – traditional costume worn in Mochudi and becoming more popular elsewhere

Room for Manoeuvre

Mma Ramotswe looked at the woman in front of her. As the newspaper photographs had suggested, she was traditionally built about the face, but also everywhere else and her dress was straining at the sides. She should move up a size or two, thought Mma Ramotswe, and then those panels on the side would not look as if they were about to rip. There really was no point in fighting these things: it is far better to admit one's size and indeed there is even a case for buying a slightly larger size. That gives room for manoeuvre.

Mma Holonga was also taking the opportunity to sum up Mma Ramotswe. Comfortable, she thought; not one of these undernourished modern ladies. That is good. But her dress is a bit tight, and she should think of getting a slightly larger size. (The Full Cupboard of Life)

As aspiring mystics may pursue an elusive enlightenment, there are some who may wonder whether they have achieved the traditional build or not, a figure that requires both time and nourishment. Others may not realise quite how traditionally built they have become and it is wise to make a pre-emptive purchase of a *Leteisi* or German-print dress, a size up. Mma Makutsi was alert to the forensic evidence of such a form and had observed Mma Ramotswe's tiny white van listing, rather notably, towards the driver's side and heard her complain of her office chair and those in Zebra Drive having become less comfortable, suspecting as she had summed it up to herself that Mma Ramotswe was 'hard on anything with springs' (*Blue Shoes and Happiness*). She had also noticed the long-term impact of the larger build upon footwear and reflected upon the excellent opportunity this must present in purchasing beautiful new shoes, when affordable.

Dieting

'Mma Ramotswe!' she exclaimed. 'If you go on a diet, then what are the rest of us to do? What will all the other traditionally built ladies think if they hear about this? How can you be so unkind?'

'Unkind?' asked Mma Ramotswe. 'I do not see how this is unkind.'

'But it is,' protested Mma Potokwani. 'Traditionally built people are always being told by other people to eat less. Their lives are often a misery. You are a well-known traditionally built person. If you go on a diet, then everybody else will feel guilty. They will feel that they have to go on a diet too, and that will spoil their lives.' (Blue Shoes and Happiness)

Mma Ramotswe has lived long enough to know that many people long to change their shape, skin colour or other feature of identity, but she also knew the sense of liberation in largely accepting who you are and being comfortable with that. However, it was the comments of others that had planted the dangerous notion of needing to go on a diet in her head. Yet her good friend, Mma Potokwani, was mortified that Mma Ramotswe, torch-bearer of the traditionally built, had succumbed to a diet so she helped return her to her senses, and to a large piece of fruitcake. The freedom of the traditionally built is to stare a seven-hundred-calorie slice of cake full in the face and know, as Mma Ramotswe knew: 'it did not matter; she was a traditionally built lady and she did not have to worry about such things' (*Morality for Beautiful Girls*). What matters is to be comfortable in one's own skin and to appreciate the important things such as family and friends, bush tea, luscious pumpkin, fine cattle, the beauty of Botswana and a sense of belonging.

Doughnuts and Dieting

A doughnut was exactly what she wanted; a doughnut with a dusting of coarse sugar on the outside, enough to give a bit of a crunch and to line one's lips with white, and a layer of sweetened oil soaked into the dough itself. Such bliss. Such bliss. (Blue Shoes and Happiness)

Doughnuts strike at the very heart of matters relating to dieting. Staring into the rumbling abyss of her own diet on day two, Mma Ramotswe herself was met with the formidable temptation of a doughnut, gifted by Phuti Radiphuti, owner of the Double Comfort Furniture Store and fiancé of Mma Makutsi. The ethics of whether it is right to eat doughnuts in the presence of one who is dieting must be a matter of personal conscience. Mma Makutsi has been sensitive to consider this issue, during Mma Ramotswe's brief time 'in the wilderness', but concluded that life must go on regardless.

Controversially, Mma Makutsi once laid claim to the slimming properties of the doughnut on account of its encompassing a circle entirely devoid of dough. Whilst this wisdom was imparted with not a little conviction, Mma Ramotswe privately doubted that the slimming area would reach anything like ninety-seven per cent, but had not pursued the point. Doughnuts have long been Mma Makutsi's reward to herself, marking the milestone of her promotion to Assistant Manager at Tlokweng Road Speedy Motors and a treat to celebrate the run-away success of the Kalahari Typing School for Men. They are best sourced from specialist outlets such as the small tuck-stand that Mma Makutsi frequents or the Bakery in Broadhurst favoured by Phuti Radiphuti. When transporting doughnuts, Mma Makutsi often took the precaution of having a magazine to hand with features on celebrity shoes and such like, merely to avoid the fat which unavoidably seeps through the paper bag.

'I see that you had doughnuts,' he said, looking pointedly at the greasy wrapping paper on the side of Mma Makutsi's desk. 'I thought doughnuts were for Friday.'

'There has been a change of policy,' said Mma Makutsi. 'A forward-looking business must be flexible.' (Tea Time for the Traditionally Built)

As tea is just the thing for client interviews, so an enlightened approach to doughnuts can be good for staff morale, substituting for team-building outings where the total number of participants, including management, would be two. Doughnuts are so comforting that they can be taken as a rescue remedy in response to a variety of situations and the *in extremis* doughnut will always be dispensed to a client in need. Indeed doughnut handling can be something of a litmus test of character in Mma Ramotswe's reckoning and she has observed with respect her assistant's fair division of doughnuts.

Rose's Fat Cakes

A Botswana speciality and traditional treat, Fat Cakes were the fore-runner to the doughnut in Botswana and remain extremely popular today. Mma Ramotswe's kitchen helper, Rose, who is an expert cook, sings as she prepares these and other delights in Mma Ramotswe's kitchen or in the covered porch where she can make a fire. Fat Cakes are made at home and brought to the office for elevenses, or purchased for one or two *pula* from stall-holders, often having entirely vanished from supermarket shelves by lunchtime.

Fat Cakes

Makes 16

Ingredients:

3 cups of cake flour
1 tsp salt
1½ tsp yeast
2 tbs sugar
¾ pint warm water
Vegetable oil to fry

Method:

Mix all ingredients well and allow to prove for 30 minutes in a warm place.
Divide dough into 16 doughnut-size pieces and deep fry until golden-brown.

Chapter 2

On the Scent of Roasting Mealies

There were hawkers at the side of the road selling rough-hewn stools and chairs, and a woman with a smoking brazier on which maize cobs were being grilled. The smell of the maize, the sharp-sweet smell that she knew so well and which spoke so much of the African roadside, wafted through the window of the tiny white van, and for a moment she was back in Mochudi, a child again, at the fireside, waiting for a cob to be passed over to her. And she saw herself all those years ago, standing away from the fire, but with the wood-smoke in her nostrils; and she was biting into the succulent maize, and thinking that this was the most perfect food that the earth had to offer. And she still thought that, all these years later, and her heart could still fill with love for that Africa that she once knew. (Blue Shoes and Happiness)

Mealies

Mealies, maize, or corn on the cob, as it is known in some parts of the world, are still cooked on fires all over Botswana. Simple and delicious, they remain a favourite of Mma Ramotswe's, their unmistakeable smell triggering childhood memories and transporting her to Mochudi. Bought from street vendors – now there is a traditional fast food – they have a smell and taste from the charcoal grill that are wholesome and connected to the earth. Braising mealies in the ash and hot embers of a fire is known as *Go besa mmidi*.

Sorghum, Maize and Millet

With a high tolerance to drought, sorghum is the traditional staple cereal crop of Botswana, nutritionally well-balanced, high in protein and gluten-free. It tastes quite sweet and is used to make what is generically referred to as 'porridge' in Botswana and is also used as flour for bread. Today, mealie meal (maize meal), imported from South Africa, is very widespread in its use. The traditional village method of milling sorghum is described on page 47, but ready-milled mealie meal/corn flour is sold everywhere in Botswana and can be purchased in African grocers elsewhere and online. Sorghum is more commonly used in the South of Botswana but heading North, beyond Serowe, the whole grain, millet, is ground and made into meal in place of sorghum.

Sorghum

Pounding sorghum for porridge using *Kika* and *Motshe*

Traditional Equipment

Kika – heavy wooden knee-high mortar used for pounding grain for porridge or flour and for crushing beans.

Motshe – giant wooden pestle used with the *Kika*.

Loselo – a shallow basket sieve made from finely woven *moretlwa* sticks, used for winnowing of grain in flour-making and to separate wheat from chaff.

Baskets

Beautiful, intricately woven baskets are one of Botswana's principal crafts and have been essential in traditional food preparation, transportation and storage for millennia. Traditionally, sorghum and other grains were stored in baskets with lids, and ingredients were transported in bowl-shaped baskets perched on a woman's head. The baskets are coil woven from the fibres of the vegetable ivory palm tree (*mokola*) and patterns added with natural dyes from indigenous plants. Made entirely by hand, a single basket can take 4 – 6 weeks to make, the valuable income coming from these sustaining families and communities in Etsha, for example, two days' drive North from Gaborone. These works of art are exported internationally by Botswanacraft Marketing[3] who work with a group of twenty weavers in Etsha to ensure that these highly skilled producers, living on small margins, receive a fair return for their artwork.

Lefetlho – wooden-handled whisk with wire loops used for mixing.

Pitsana e Maoto a mararo – huge three-legged cauldrons, also called *Falkirks*, they were imported from South Africa and Zimbabwe. Today they are mainly used for large celebrations such as weddings and harvest festivals. These metal pots were preceded by clay ones which have been made by women in Botswana for thousands of years. They were also used in villages for water storage and in fermenting sorghum to make local beer.

Lerotse or *lekatane* porridge, stirred with a *lefetlho*, whisk

Bogobe and *Phaletshe* – **Porridge**

Porridge is a mainstay of cooking and eating in Botswana, made either from sorghum or maize to produce *Bogobe* and *Phaletshe* respectively. Maize has long been imported from South Africa where mealie meal is known as *pap* (and as *ugali* in East Africa).

Porridge

Recipes and methods of preparation vary from tribe to tribe and there are many different Setswana names for different variations. In the past, *Bogobe* was often the main course itself in many tribes and it is still enjoyed on its own with a relish. Today *Bogobe* and *Phaletshe* are commonly eaten in the same way that rice or potatoes are in some other parts of the world, as an accompaniment.

Thin, soft sorghum porridge, *Motogo*, makes a filling start to the day and thicker *Mosoko* is eaten for lunch or an evening meal with meat, when finances permit. Porridge cooked with Setswana melon (*lerotse* or *lekatane*) is also a favourite, when these local cooking melons are in season. *Ting* or sour porridge is extremely popular. Sour milk is added to plain porridge or the melon variety while it is still cooking or afterwards. When added to plain porridge it is called *Sebube. Bogobe* and *Phaletshe* are cooked on stove-tops and wood fires all over the country.

Three products are made from maize: mealie meal, mealie rice and samp. All of these are now widely available, ready prepared and packaged and are made from the 'polished' or cracked maize kernels, dehulled and broken down, traditionally with the giant mortar and pestle to different sizes of granule, samp remaining the largest and mealie rice the finest.

Phaletshe (Mealie Meal)

Ingredients:

10 tbs of mealie meal
3 cups cold water
½ tsp salt (optional)

Method:

Mix the mealie meal with a little cold water to make a paste. Add more cold water so that you are easily able to pour it into a pot of boiling water. Add salt and stir, making sure that there aren't any lumps. Reduce heat to a simmer, cover the pot and let it cook 15–20 minutes. Stir occasionally. Add water if necessary. The consistency needs to be thick, so that when you squeeze a handful in your palm it will easily form a semi-solid ball.

Motogo (Soft Porridge)

Ingredients:

3 heaped tbs of sorghum meal
3 cups cold water (or water mixed with milk)
½ tsp salt

Method:

Mix the sorghum meal with a little cold water to make a paste. Add more cold water so that you are easily able to pour it into a pot of boiling water. Add salt and stir, making sure that there aren't any lumps. Reduce heat to a simmer, cover the pot and let it cook 15–20 minutes. Stir occasionally. Add water if necessary. For this porridge, the consistency needs to be soft, similar to oatmeal porridge. It can be eaten at breakfast with a little additional milk and sugar, to taste.

Samp

Samp

An alternative maize product, samp is made from 'polished' or 'cracked' mealie kernels.

It goes very nicely with stew and can be bought packaged and ready to use, but is traditionally prepared by de-hulling the mealie kernels with the Setswana mortar and pestle. Samp is as comforting as a great big traditional cuddle, Mma Ramotswe often thought.

To prepare samp, boil and then simmer, as you would for rice, until tender, approximately 40 minutes.

Mosutlhane or Mosarwa (Polished Sorghum)

Remove the coloured husks from the grain by pounding the soaked sorghum.

De-chaff, take out broken particles and leave only whole grains.

Wash thoroughly in water by rubbing grain between palms.

Cook as you would for rice, until tender. Add a little salt and oil. It can also be eaten with milk.

Morula fruit may be added to the *mosutlhane*.

Dikgobe (Samp and Beans)

Ingredients:

2 cups samp

½ cup dried beans (brown or white)

Enough water to cover the samp and beans

Method:

Soak samp and beans overnight. Boil the samp for about 40 minutes.

Add beans and cook for another hour. Add salt and oil or butter to taste.

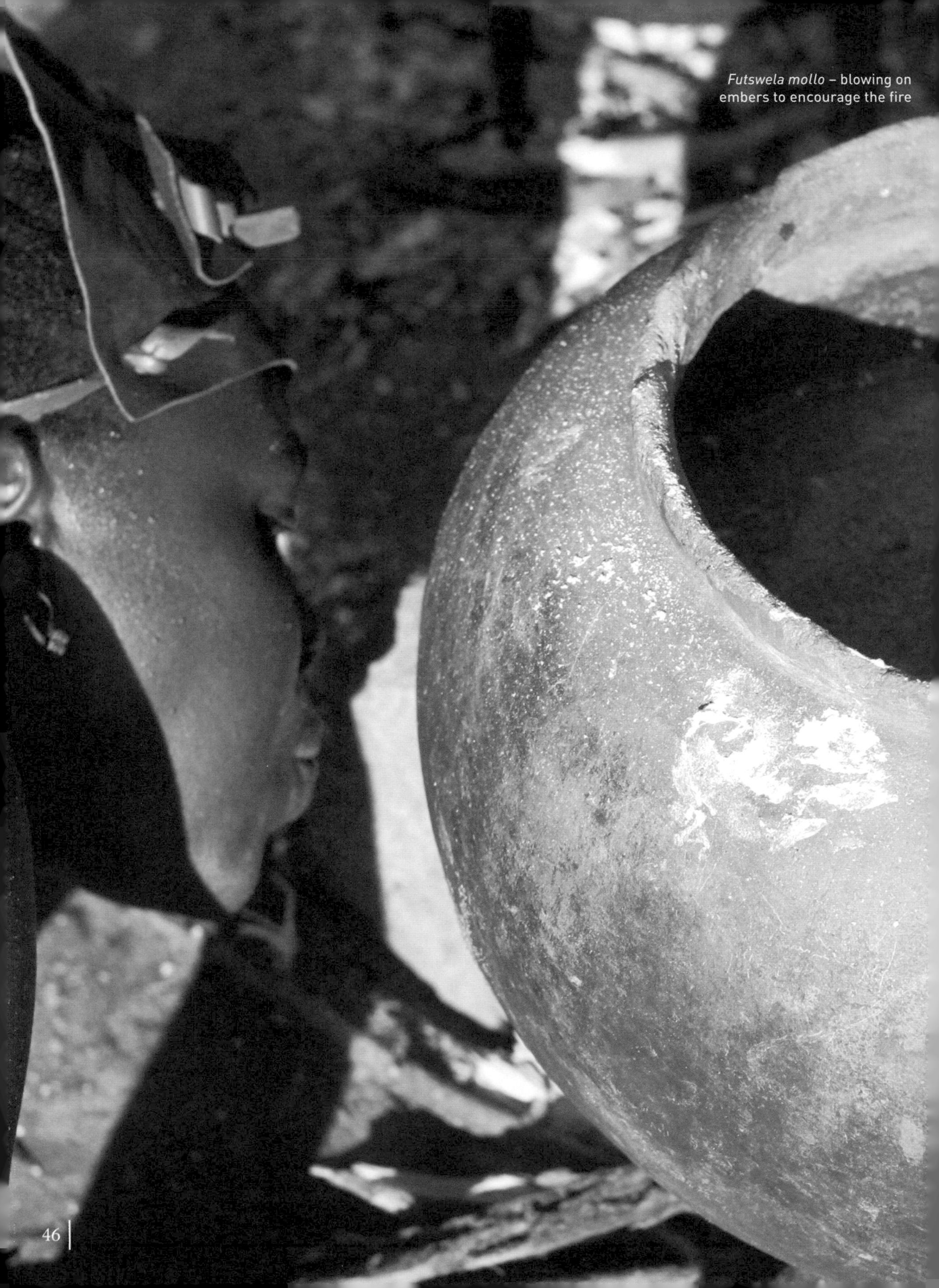

Futswela mollo – blowing on embers to encourage the fire

Futswela mollo is the Setswana term for blowing on the embers to bring on a fire, at the expense of stinging eyes. The clouds of woodsmoke that perfume the warm evening air and the crackle and glow of open fires still transport the owner of Botswana's only female detective agency back to childhood and evoke a sense of goodness, a full stomach and feeling safe in a way that words could never hint at. In her mind's eye there would be clusters of fires burning at a distance from the *Lelwapa*, the stone-floored preparation and winnowing area that was a blur of activity. Precious herself, under the watchful eye of the *Kgosana*, the Subordinate Chief and other ladies who all seemed very old and were seated on the low surrounding wall, had learned the different steps of this time- and energy- intensive process. This was a world and a lifetime apart from fast food.

In common with the other girls in Mochudi, Precious began learning to cook around the age of five. In those days, village girls became largely self-sufficient by seven, enabling the women to undertake more work in the fields or tend to the younger children and livestock. By perhaps ten or eleven, they were required to have achieved a level of skill such that they would be responsible for preparing their parents' meal. Mr J.L.B. Matekoni knew from Mma Potokwani that the House Mothers at the Orphan Farm started teaching the children to cook from an early age and she said that they often began with simple recipes for bread, scones and small cakes before moving on to the stews, *seswaa* and other savoury mainstays of everyday eating in Botswana.

Lekatane Porridge

To make *Lekatane* porridge in the traditional way, a Setswana melon is sliced and put into a pot of boiling water on the wood fire. Meanwhile, sorghum is softened in a pot of water (this steeping process known as *kolobetsa mabele*) and then sifted in a large, round, shallow traditional basket, a *loselo*. This takes place over a special mat made from cow, goat or sheepskin, called a *phate*. The sorghum is then ground by an energetic stamping, known as *thuga*, where two ladies work together, pounding the sorghum in a turn-about, rhythmical effort. The sorghum is pulverised in a knee-high wooden mortar or *kika*, made from a hollowed-out tree trunk, and using a six-foot wooden pestle, the *motshe*. This takes skill, strength and stamina and would, thought Mma Ramotswe, test the mettle of any of the modern-build gym ladies with their regimes, funny shorts and heart attack alarms. Ladies watching from

their work-stations at the pots and others by the *lelwapa* would often sing a *gareja* – a song of encouragement. The land-locked equivalent of a sea-shanty, the *gareja* is a cheeky song in which singers acknowledge that when the work of the pounding is to be done, there are only two involved, but that when it comes to the eating, many people suddenly materialise. Ladies around the world would surely nod and sigh at this.

Beans are released from their pods using the *Kika* and *Motshe*

48

In the kitchen at the back of the house there was a packet of green beans that needed to be washed and chopped. There was a pumpkin that was not going to cook itself. There were onions to be put in a pan of boiling water and cooked until soft. That was part of being a woman, she thought; one never reached the end. Even if one could sit down and drink a cup of bush tea, or even two cups, one always knew that at the end of the tea somebody was waiting for something. Children or men were waiting to be fed; a dirty floor cried out to be washed; a crumpled skirt called for the iron. And so it would continue . . .

(Blue Shoes and Happiness)

The sorghum is then returned to the *lelwapa* where it is winnowed (*go fefere*) in the *loselo*. Today the chaff is kept for the still ubiquitous chickens, but in years gone by, before refined white flour, would have been used to make bread. The mixture is then returned to the *kika* for more energy-intensive milling with the *motshe* before coming back for more sieving, which is known at this stage in the process as *tshe tshe tha*. Once satisfied that the chaff has been removed, the flour is mixed in a bowl by hand and poured into the pot of melon and boiling water. The pot has to be seen to be bubbling – *pitsana ya kgakgatha*. The pot is mixed using a whisk, or *lefetlho* which is operated by rolling its wooden handle between the palms of the hands (see p.42).

Dried Setswana beans (similar to black-eye beans), still in their pods, which can be stored for a year, are then gently tamped down and crushed using the *kika* and *motshe* to release the beans from their pods. The contents are moved in a basket and skilfully allowed to fall to the threshing floor in a winnowing process known as *olosa*. Any breeze carries the chaff away and, in the absence of a breath of wind, the heavier beans separate themselves, settling at the bottom of the pile. This technique might look to outsiders like a hopelessly inefficient process, but in expert hands is an impressively effective practice and the beans are added to the *lerotse* or *lekatane* pot in plenty.

For a lunch or evening meal, the *lerotse* porridge might be served with boiled chicken (see p.107) and *Morogo wa dinawa* (see p.51), the leaves of the common Setswana bean, which tastes not unlike spinach. After being picked, the bean leaves are parboiled and dried and can be purchased from stall-holders by the cupful as small fat squares that are then put into boiling water for ten minutes, but which can be embellished with a tasty recipe. The ladies who keep these stalls are invariably traditionally built and are implacable pillars in the life and landscape of Botswana, watchful and knowing.

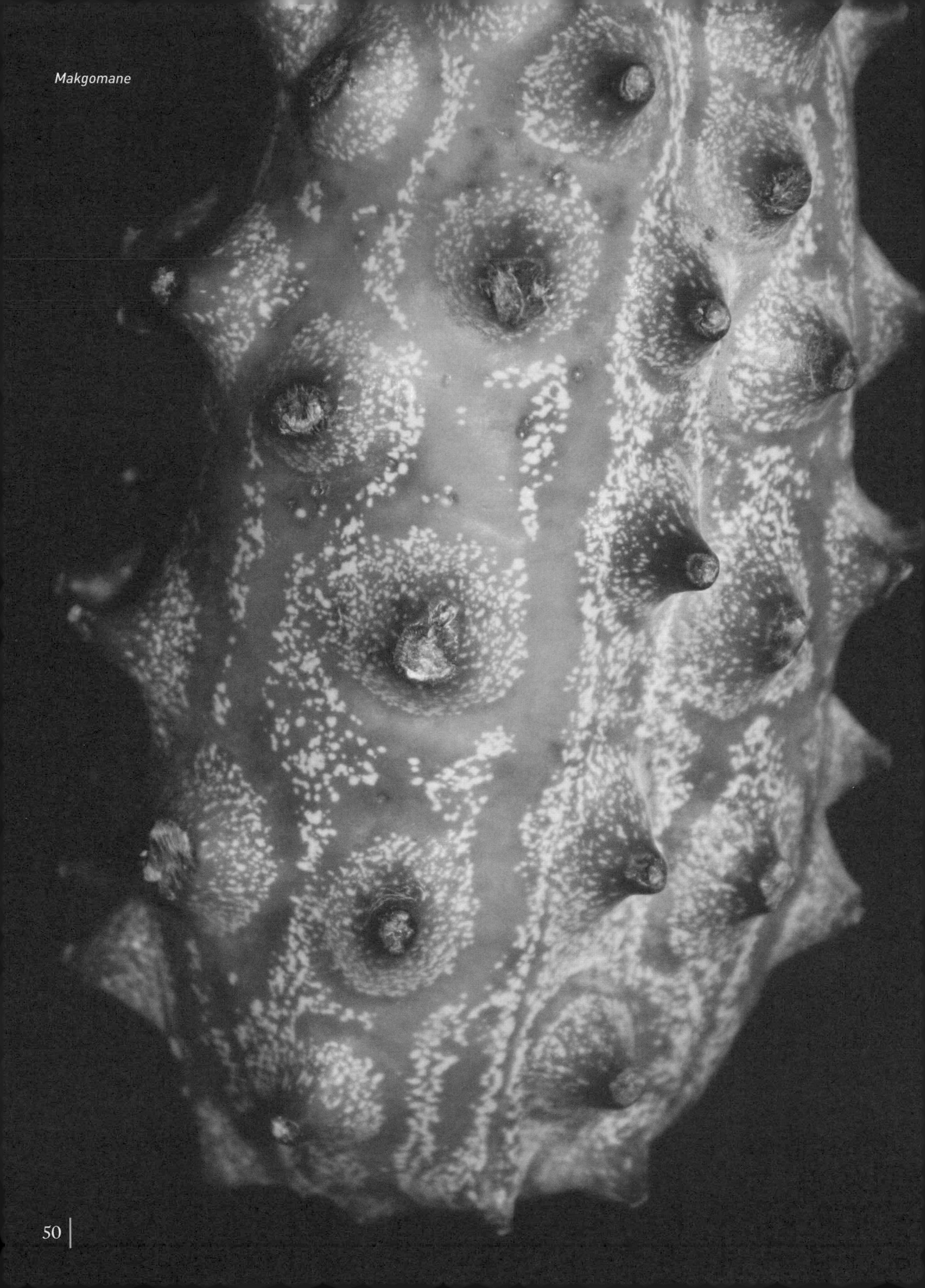

Everything was based on trust . . . buying the food from a roadside vendor, whom you trusted not to poison you.

(The Full Cupboard of Life)

Morogo (Dried Bean Leaf)

This recipe will feed 4 people. Often eaten with *phaletshe* (mealie meal) or rice.

Ingredients:

6 cups dried bean leaves

6 fresh *morula* fruits where the skin is still green

4 fresh tomatoes

1 fresh onion

2 cups of cubed pumpkin (pumpkin is diced into sugar cube sizes)

½ tsp of sugar

¼ tsp salt

1 cube vegetable stock

4 tbs cooking oil

Method:

Rinse the dried bean leaves in a bowl of water to remove any residual sand particles and drain well. Crush and break into small pieces. Add the *morula* fruit whole and boil the leaves in ½ a cup of water in a spacious saucepan with the lid on. Once the skin of the *morula* fruit is soft, remove the fruit from the saucepan and continue boiling the leaves until most of the water has evaporated. Finely chop the onion, add oil to the bean leaves and fry until the onions are soft or browned. Place the tomatoes in a bowl of boiling water for a couple of minutes to remove the skins, finely chop and add to the bean leaves. Add the sugar, the vegetable stock, the salt and the pumpkin and leave to simmer at low heat for 10–15 minutes until the pumpkin is soft.

Makgomane

A green vegetable marrow, about the size of a grapefruit, the *makgomane* is shaped like a butternut squash, its skin covered in little bumps. *Makgomane* are so delicious when young that one can eat the whole thing, including the seeds and skin.

Method:

Clean and cut into either two or four parts; boil in a little water until soft and serve as an additional dish either at lunch or dinner. Alternatively: when soft, mash till smooth and add some fresh or sour milk (*madila*).

Delele

Serves 8

Typical in the North of the country, *delele* has spinach-like leaves and is slimy in texture when cooked. Best prepared with bicarbonate of soda, it was traditionally made with water to which a little of the ash from the fire had been added.

Ingredients:

1 lb 2 oz *delele* leaves (fresh or dried)	2 oz cherry tomatoes (chopped)
2 oz onion (chopped)	1 oz bicarbonate of soda
Salt	4 cups of water

Method:

To a saucepan add 4 cups of water, salt and the bicarbonate of soda.
Bring to the boil and add the *delele*.
Add the tomato and onion and simmer, beating occasionally so that the mixture does not froth.
Cook for 15 minutes or until the mixture blends well.
Serve hot with *phaletshe* or *bogobe*.

Thepe or Rothwe with Groundnuts

Thepe and *Rothwe* are seasonal spinach-like plants.

Method:

Clean and cook *thepe* for approximately 10 – 15 minutes in a little water (*rothwe* takes a little longer to cook than *thepe*). Add tomato and chillies if desired. Drain the water and mash the *thepe* until smooth. Add a small quantity of groundnuts to the pot and stir. Add a pinch of salt and leave on the fire/hob for about 4 or 5 minutes more. Serve with *phaletshe* for lunch or an evening meal.

Cabbage with Groundnuts and Tomatoes

Serves 6

Ingredients:

1 cabbage	4 chopped tomatoes
½ cup pounded groundnuts (peanuts)	½ tsp salt

Method:

Wash the cabbage leaves and cut into small pieces. Bring a small amount of water to boil in a pot, add the salt and cabbage. Add the tomatoes and the groundnuts, stirring on a low heat until only a little liquid remains. It is ready when the cabbage is soft with 'a little bite' on the thicker parts.

Beans

Sugar beans and red kidney beans grow well in the North of Botswana. Cowpeas or black-eye peas (a subspecies of black-eye beans) are very popular. Tswana cowpeas grow well in most parts of Botswana as they weather drought conditions well as do *Ditloo* beans. China beans (*letlhodi*) are another staple variety.

Black-eye Bean Patties

Serves 2

Ingredients:

1 cup beans	1 cup flour
1 tsp baking powder	1 small onion
1 medium tomato (ripe or half ripe)	

Method:

Cook the beans in water until soft. Mash thoroughly. Allow to cool and add the flour and baking powder. Cut the onion into thin slices and add to the mixture. Cut the tomato into the mixture and blend well. Shape into 'cookies' and fry in hot fat.

Ditloo le Letshotlo

Serves 6

Ingredients:

14 oz *Ditloo* beans

14 oz *letshotlo* (fresh mealies, boiled and dried)

Salt and pepper to taste

2 oz butter

Method:

Mix the beans and mealies and soak overnight in water.

Place mixture in saucepan and add fresh water.

Bring to the boil and then reduce heat to simmer until the mixture is thoroughly cooked.

Add the butter and season to taste.

Simmer until the mixture blends well.

Serve hot, alone or as accompaniment to beef or chicken dishes.

Pumpkin: a favourite of Mma Ramotswe

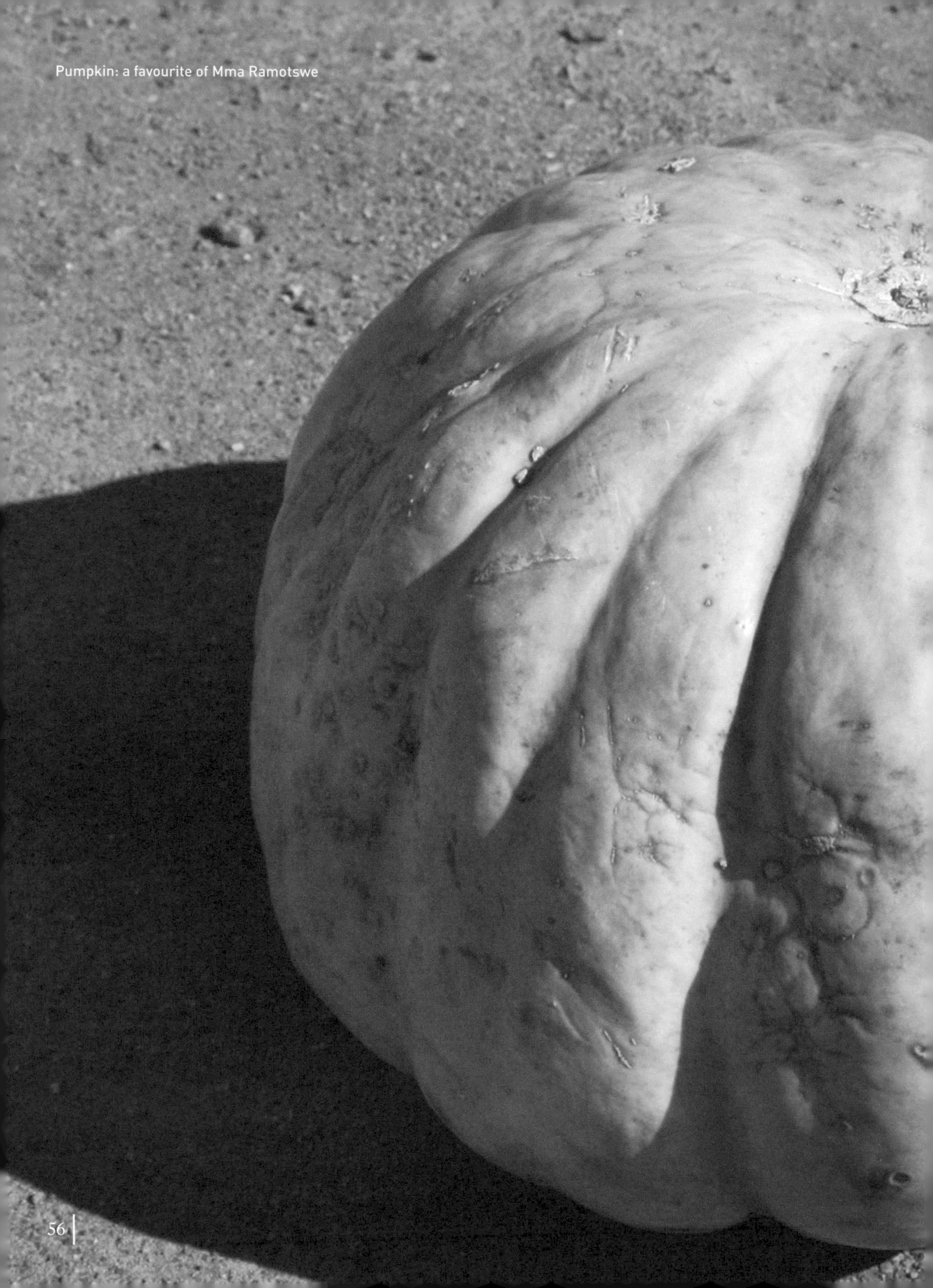

The yellow flesh of a pumpkin or a squash, boiled and then softened with a lump of butter (if one's budget stretched to that) was one of God's greatest gifts to Botswana. And it tasted so good too, with a slice of fine Botswana beef, dripping in gravy. (The Full Cupboard of Life)

Mma Ramotswe is a great champion of the pumpkin, particularly large ripened ones that follow the rainy season, which are just right for traditionally built ladies. A good pumpkin reveals itself when you pick it up. If it is heavy, then it is ready, and weight is more important than size in pumpkins, as with melons. The white pumpkins are nice, but Mma Ramotswe favours the round, greenish ones which have such flavour. Prepared as a side vegetable, pumpkin can also be steamed or roasted with its skin on, which, like the jackets of baked potatoes, contains much goodness. They can also be peeled or mashed with butter.

Pumpkin Leaves with Tomato and Onion

Serves 2

Ingredients:

A bunch of tenderest pumpkin leaves	4 tomatoes cut into rings
Salt and red pepper	Cooking oil
¾ cup water	1 onion, sliced

Method:

Clean the leaves thoroughly. Strip the thickest fibres from the stems and leaves. Cut the leaves and stems into desired size. Boil the water in a saucepan, adding salt and pepper. Add pumpkin leaves and cover tightly. Simmer until pumpkin leaves are cooked then drain off the water. Fry onion in the oil until soft, add the tomatoes and cook for 5 minutes. Add this mixture to the pumpkin leaves and cook for another 5 minutes. Serve.

Pumpkin Leaves with Groundnuts

Serves 2

Ingredients:

A bunch of tender pumpkin leaves (add ½ tsp bicarbonate of soda to the pumpkin leaves if they are not very young, to soften them).

1 sliced onion	3 chopped tomatoes
Salt and pepper	3 tbs of groundnuts, or peanut butter

Method:

Clean leaves and cut into small pieces. Boil ½ cup water and add salt to it. Add pumpkin leaves. Lower heat to simmer. When leaves are slightly cooked add the onion, tomatoes and pounded groundnuts. Add pepper. Cook for 10 – 15 minutes more, stirring occasionally. Serve.

Squash and pumpkin are favourites in Zebra Drive

Steamed Pumpkin Slices

Serves 6

Ingredients:

Pumpkin

Water

Salt

Sugar (optional)

Butter

Method:

To steam, place slices of pumpkin in a pan with a little water, salt (and sugar, if you love your sugar as Mma Ramotswe does). Cover with a lid, ensuring that the water does not all evaporate. Cook for 30 – 40 minutes until the outer skin is soft (the greenish pumpkin has a thicker skin). Serve with butter.

The mystery of life! thought Mma Ramotswe. The mystery of pumpkins. Why are pumpkins the shape they are? Why is the flesh of the pumpkin the colour it is? Can anybody explain that, or is it just something that is? Again she struggled to stop her train of thought and concentrated on what Trevor Mwamba was saying. (In the Company of Cheerful Ladies)

Roasting pumpkin slices in the oven takes longer and as with baked potatoes they can be cooked in tin foil or not, depending on how you like the skin. Either way, you must put some dots of butter on the skin to avoid it drying out too much. It is very tasty baked in foil with a little bit of cinnamon stick or ground cinnamon sprinkled over the butter. Pumpkins can also make lovely soup or fritters. One of Motholeli's favourites, pumpkin is among the repertoire that she and Puso and Mr J.L.B. Matekoni have cooked for Mma Ramotswe.

Mma Ramotswe was greatly impressed when Mrs Moffat explained how a great Scottish writer, Rra Burns, who is now late, had written a poem honouring a Scottish dish and that school students today all read about the haggis. The pumpkin deserves similar treatment and her countrymen could put on a suitable spectacle, Mma Ramotswe reflected, one in which Mr J.L.B. Matekoni could play a quietly heroic role. But sometimes it is enough to celebrate things without too much fanfare. To appreciate delicious, ripe pumpkin by enjoying it with family or friends, that is enough.

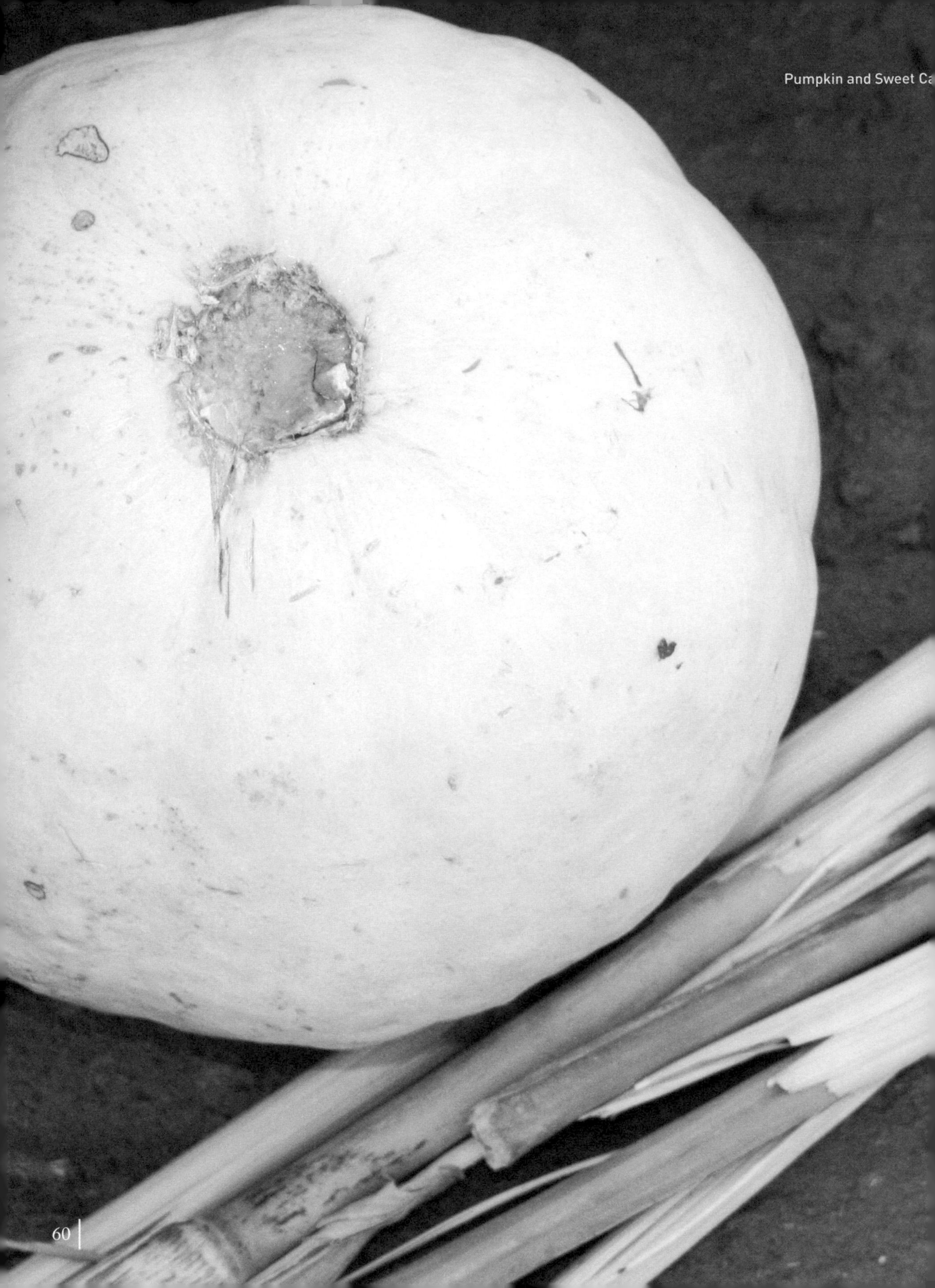

Curried Pumpkin Soup

Serves 6

Ingredients:

2 lb 4 oz pumpkin flesh (no skin or pips), roughly chopped

1 large potato, peeled and roughly chopped

1 large onion, chopped finely

1 tsp medium or hot curry powder

4 cups water

Salt, pepper and sugar to taste

2 skinned, seeded and roughly chopped tomatoes

Method:

Place prepared vegetables in a large pot. Add curry powder and water and bring to the boil, stirring occasionally. Reduce heat, cover and simmer for 20 – 25 minutes or until vegetables are very tender. Remove from heat. Spoon mixture carefully into an electric blender and blend until smooth. Return to pot, add salt, pepper and sugar to taste. Bring back to boil, stirring frequently. Thin down with extra boiling water if necessary.

It was time to take the pumpkin out of the pot and eat it. In the final analysis, that was what solved these big problems in life. You could think and think and get nowhere, but you still had to eat your pumpkin. That gave you a reason for going on (The No. 1 Ladies' Detective Agency)

Butternut Soup

Serves 6

Especially good for an evening, this soup doesn't take long to make.

Ingredients:

2 lb butternut	**3 potatoes**
1 onion (white or red), chopped	**½ oz butter**
6 tsp chicken stock powder	**4 cups cold water**

Method:

Dice the butternut and potatoes and mix together. Melt butter in pan and soften vegetables in it. Add the water and stock powder and cook for 40 minutes.

Traditional pottery is made in Gabane

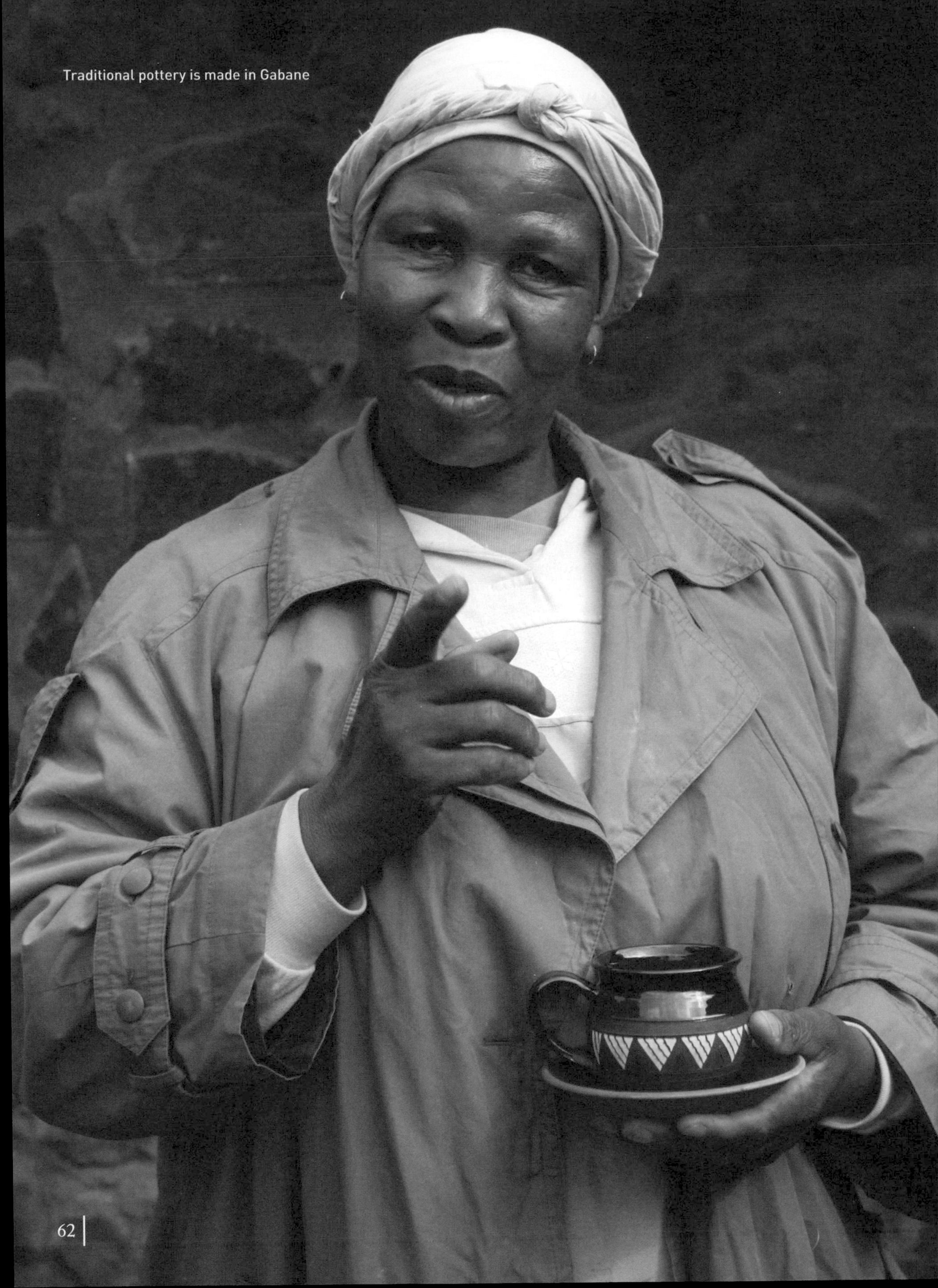

You Clever Men, You Can Cook Too!

Mma Ramotswe had never seen Mr J.L.B. Matekoni touch the kettle in all the six months since their marriage and his arrival in the house in Zebra Drive. Mr J.L.B. Matekoni liked tea, of course – it would have been very difficult to marry a man who did not like tea – but he very rarely seemed to make any tea for himself. She had not thought about this before now, but it was rather interesting, was it not, that somebody might believe that tea just happened along? Mr J.L.B. Matekoni was not a lazy man, but it was remarkable to reflect how most men imagined that things like tea and food would simply appear if they waited long enough. There would always be a woman in the background – a mother, a girlfriend, a wife – who would ensure that these needs would be met. This should change, of course, and men should learn how to look after themselves, but very few men seemed to be doing this yet. And there was not much hope for the younger generation, looking at the two apprentices and how they behaved. They still expected women to look after them and, unfortunately, there seemed to be enough young women who were prepared to do this. (In the Company of Cheerful Ladies)

Though an old Setswana poem has women first ploughing the earth and then making the food, Mma Ramotswe is not content with this level of female servitude and the lifetime of cooking that had traditionally been ascribed to the role of women. Some men were trying hard, she thought, and the situation in towns had improved a lot, but others, especially in villages, remained fugitive from the division of labour reasonable in a modern marriage, quite content for women to do the work.

If men were to be swept aside, wondered Phuti Radiphuti, then where would men be put? Would there be special homes for them, where they could be given small tasks to perform while women got on with the important business of running things? (Blue Shoes and Happiness)

Like 'big men' enthroned behind the tinted glass of their expensive imported vehicles, these men would hide behind the smoke screen of 'the old ways' to evade domestic responsibility, even writing off cooking as 'woman's work'. Mma Potokwani and Mma Ramotswe share the wish that these culprits could spend some time working in the President Hotel, or the Gaborone Sun Hotel alongside Cedric Motoposipe's brother and one of the sons of the woman who swept Mma Ramotswe's office. There they would learn of the discipline, skill and stamina required to succeed in such professional kitchens.

Cooking a Little More Often than Sometimes

Mr J.L.B. Matekoni here is only a man. He cannot be expected to keep his own house clean ... If you have been feeding him so well, then why is he so thin? A man who is well looked-after becomes fatter. They are just like cattle. That is well known. (Tears of the Giraffe)

Dr Maketsi was one, Mma Ramotswe remembered, who had managed to side-step any discussion of emancipation and given her the slip when she had sought to ask him what he liked to cook. She knew from a friend's daughter who had recently returned from America that she had caught the doctor off-guard and challenged him: 'If you eat, you should cook. It's as simple as that'! (*The No. 1 Ladies' Detective Agency*) at which point he had assumed all the authority of his position and looked at her with professional scepticism. It was strange that such views could persist, particularly taking into account how highly revered that Doctor's aunt, a retired teacher, was. Clearly her nephew was one of the few who didn't turn to her for advice. Hector Mapondise had a little more insight into the psyche of the modern female detective, thought Mma Ramotswe wistfully, as when proposing for the second time, he had sought to woo her with the promise of a cook, or two cooks and the assurance: 'You could still be a detective' (*The No. 1 Ladies' Detective Agency*), but a man that she struggled to maintain consciousness around was not someone with whom she could contemplate spending a lifetime.

... 'And I do not have to cook any more,' added Mr J.L.B. Matekoni.

'But you never did cook, Rra,' said Mma Potokwani. 'What is this talk about cooking?'

'I sometimes cooked,' said Mr J.L.B. Matekoni.

'When did you cook?' asked Mma Potokwani.

'Sometimes,' said Mr J.L.B. Matekoni. 'But we must not stand around and talk about cooking. I must go and fix this pump of yours.' (The Kalahari Typing School for Men)

Mma Ramotswe thought with fondness, how dear men need to be properly cared for, the very antithesis of the treatment that Mr J.L.B. Matekoni had been receiving from his lazy kitchen helper, Florence. Mma Ramotswe had no trouble in being direct where it was called for and had challenged the recalcitrant Florence that if thus treated 'our men would have died out a long time ago'. Prior to getting married, Mma Ramotswe eagerly anticipated being able to show signs of love for Mr J.L.B. Matekoni by cooking for and looking after him. As she expressed it:

'We do need somebody else in this life ... we need a person whom we can make our little god on this earth' (Morality for Beautiful Girls)

and in married life, Mma Ramotswe is happy in the practice of this devotion.

Supporting Men

She glanced at Mr J.L.B. She knew that men of his age started to feel trapped and began to wonder if this was all that life offered. It was understandable; anyone might feel that, not just men, although they might feel it particularly acutely, as they felt themselves weaken and began to realise that they were no longer young. Women were better at coming to terms with that, thought Mma Ramotswe, as long as they were not the worrying sort. If one was of traditional build and not given to fretting . . . If one drank plenty of bush tea . . .

(The Good Husband of Zebra Drive)

Mr J.L.B. Matekoni was the paragon of a steady man. However, providing him with all the good food she gave her husband still afforded Mma Ramotswe some peace of mind, knowing that he wouldn't leave her for a 'newer model' as it seemed to her men were so prone to do nowadays.

Mrs Moffat had agreed that this was indeed a good way of keeping a man. Men clearly had more trouble with age than woman, Mma Ramotswe often thought; firstly in apparently struggling to grow up. Their 'inner child', to whom Clovis Andersen had alluded in that seminal work, *The Principles of Private Detection*, often seemed to need so much more attention than 'inner girls'. Mma Makutsi, who often spoke sharply to the two Apprentices, would have had little truck with this. Girls just matured so much faster, everyone knew that, they really did. From an early age, girls had to get on with looking after younger children and men, as well as cooking and the beginnings of the seemingly endless list of tasks that faced women. Men also had difficulty in coming to terms with their outer appearance, being apparently at odds with how they felt within.

Many of the women who came to see her were worried about their middle-aged husbands, and Mma Ramotswe had read somewhere about the male menopause and all the troubles to which it gave rise. (Blue Shoes and Happiness)

Men could be so much less expressive. This was a topic of conversation that had come up between Mma Makutsi and Mma Ramotswe in one of their daily discussions first thing in the morning. These took place after the first, unofficial cup of tea when there was an exchange of information; Mr J.L.B. Matekoni and Radio Botswana would be quoted and there would be a report on what Mma Makutsi had cooked for Phuti Radiphuti.

Mr J.L.B. Matekoni was one of these men who have a tendency to be less expressive than women. It was sometimes difficult to know exactly what was going on inside this sensible but sensitive man and Mma Ramotswe wanted to be an emotional safety net for him. The gravitational effects of the traditional build were grounding, and ladies with the robust constitution and philosophical outlook that came with the achievement and maintenance of this build were better prepared to deal with life's ups and downs. There are many dishes in this book which can support men, particularly the meat ones which they might be encouraged to imagine that they had themselves provided, with their bare hands. On more than one occasion, Mma Ramotswe had observed a strangely distant expression come over Mr J.L.B. Matekoni as he picked up his old hunting knife. He remarked with a dreamy tone that its sharp blade was good for tackling meat.

The Modern Traditional Man Who Cooks

. . . the thought filled her with gratitude that she had such a man who would think to cook a meal. Most husbands would never do that – would regard it as beneath their dignity to work in the house – but Mr J.L.B. Matekoni was different. It was as if he knew what it was like to be a woman, to have all that cooking to do, for the rest of one's life, a whole procession of pots and pans stretching out into the distance, seemingly endless. Women knew all about that, and dreamed about cooking and pots and the like, but here was a man who seemed to understand.

(The Full Cupboard of Life)

Mr J.L.B. Matekoni, who may have been Botswana's finest mechanic, was a typical Motswana being, at heart a farmer who found peace tending his vegetable garden and in sharing Mma Ramotswe's love of cattle. She was very lucky, thought Mma Ramotswe, to have a husband who was such a good man and who respected her and didn't spend all of his time in bars drinking beer, as some did. She knew that he admired her work, as Botswana's No. 1 lady detective, particularly having himself experienced some of its challenges. Mr J.L.B. Matekoni had praised her as a great cook and observed her versatility in being best at cooking pumpkins but also being able to bake cakes. Such was his faith in her that given the chance, he believed Mma Ramotswe could even 'run Botswana'. In turn she loved this dear, gentle man. She was delighted that Mr J.L.B. Matekoni, together with the children, cooked a meal for her, prior to a difficult conversation about his having agreed to do a parachute jump, yet this was something of a flash in the pan as Mr J.L.B. Matekoni had previously shown little interest in cooking.

Ever watchful for signs of a return of the depressive illness that had sometimes dogged Mr J.L.B. Matekoni as it does so many fine and gifted people, Mma Ramotswe continued to reflect upon ways to shield the spirit of this kind and sensitive man. Depression, Mma Ramotswe had learned from Dr Moffat, was an illness entirely divorced from feeling a little down, but which descended with the speed of darkness falling in Africa and could be as confining as dense acacia. It stole appetite and any sort of savour, Mma Ramotswe had quickly observed. Mma Potokwani who had been a great support, helping nurse Mr J.L.B. Matekoni through this time had suggested that finding additional activities that were meditative and which took Mr J.L.B. Matekoni out of himself, whilst not a defence, might offer some additional self-nourishment.

Mma Ramotswe knew from experience that Mr J.L.B. Matekoni's own meditations often seemed to centre around solving mechanical problems; he was so good with his hands. And it was this reflection upon Mr J.L.B. Matekoni's large mechanic's hands (like those of her cousin's husband, whom she remembered from childhood) that led Mma Ramotswe to plant the seed in Mr J.L.B. Matekoni's head that he might from time to time make bread and perhaps bake with the children. Mma Ramotswe had heard from a wise neighbour in Gaborone that Lady Khama had made lovely brown bread and wondered whether her husband had ever baked.

The First President of Botswana, H.E., Sir Seretse Khama & Lady Khama: much admired and remembered with respect by Mma Ramotswe

Much excellent produce is grown in Botswana

Whilst he would probably have described himself as a simple mechanic, Mr J.L.B. Matekoni was not by any means unaffected by smell. He loved Mma Ramotswe's own bouquet that was somehow Botswana in essence; the distinctive smell of wood smoke, the sweet breath of cattle, oil and metal from a healthy engine, the thrilling lungful of pristine upholstery, the dangerous intoxicating aroma of Mma Potokwani's fruitcake and amongst the most reassuring and homely, the smell of baking bread that transported him back to his own childhood. Mr J.L.B. Matekoni wondered what his own father, Pumphamilitse Matekoni, farmer and chief caretaker of the Railway Head Office, might have made of him baking bread and reflected that this decent man would have approved of anything that his son chose to do that was based upon fairness and honest effort.

It was important to use the right tools for any job but also to practise some favouritism. Under closer inspection, a little extra wear would perhaps have been visible in Tlokweng Road Speedy Motors on a trusted spanner that felt just right in the hand. Similarly, there had been occasions when Mr J.L.B. Matekoni had had to rescue a favourite jacket or pair of trousers – faithful retainers which Mma Ramotswe didn't recognise as having vital signs of further service. For bread-making, Mr J.L.B. Matekoni had fashioned a fine breadboard out of a beautiful piece of acacia wood that he had been keeping in the recesses of his workshop until its purpose became clear.

Mr J.L.B. Matekoni liked making the sort of bread he enjoyed eating, the variety that had some personality. The process of creating something always felt satisfying, and he enjoyed the stages of building something up and the patience that was required for bread in kneading, proving, rising and baking. Beyond being a breadwinner in the financial sense, shoulder to shoulder with Mma Ramotswe, it felt good to provide for the family table in a palpable way, be it the beautiful mottled beans from his vegetable patch or the physical form of a loaf that you could hold in your hands. Mr J.L.B. Matekoni's bread was enjoyed thickly cut by Motholeli, spread with jam for breakfast. It was also adopted as the office cupboard loaf, although he sometimes questioned whether the bread could be tasted, given the thickness of the jam that Mma Makutsi and Mma Ramotswe applied.

Mealie Bread

Ingredients:

3 cups grated mealies

1 cup flour

3 tsp baking powder

1 tbs sugar

1 tsp salt

1 tbs oil

Method:

Cook the mealies (maize/corn on the cob) and grate the kernels off the cob (instead of cutting them off and then mincing them). Mix all the ingredients together. Put into a greased tin and bake in a medium oven (180°C) 45 minutes.

Flatbreads cooked over an open fire on the upturned lid of a large 3-legged pot

Flatbreads over a Wood Fire

Long ago, the sorghum chaff would have been used to make a high fibre bread (*Diphaphatha tsa moroko*). It was moistened with traditional beer, instead of yeast, to make it rise. Refined white flour and instant yeast sachets have been widely available in Botswana for many years, even in villages distant from population concentrations and the white flour versions are called *Duba-borotho*.

To make the bread, the moist dough is kneaded and fashioned into round patties by passing it from one palm to the next, *Diphaphatha* (literally, clapping). The roundels of bread are then baked on a large up-turned pot lid that has been placed on the fire to make a girdle or griddle.

Sorghum Bread

Ingredients:

1 cup sorghum flour
1 tbs sugar
½ tsp salt
½ tbs yeast
¼ cup lukewarm water
1 cup boiling water
2½ cups plain flour

Method:

Sift sorghum flour, sugar and salt together and mix this with 1 cup boiling water. Sprinkle the yeast over ¼ cup lukewarm water. Let both mixtures stand for about 10 minutes. Stir the yeast solution into the sorghum mixture then stir in the 2½ cups flour. Mix and knead the dough until soft and elastic. Put into a greased bowl. Cover and let rise until double in size. Re-knead and shape into loaves and put into greased tins and cover. When doubled in size, bake for 30 – 45 minutes at 170ºC.

The San Bushmen of the Kalahari traditionally live close to nature and the land

The San Bushmen

'You must understand,' said Mma Potokwani, 'that when you look at the life they lead, out there in the Kalahari, with no cattle of their own and no houses to live in; when you think about that and wonder how long you and I and other Batswana would be able to live like that, then you realise that these bushmen are remarkable people.' (Tears of the Giraffe)

Mr J.L.B. Matekoni and Mma Ramotswe greatly admired the San Bushmen and would gently encourage their foster child Puso to take a pride in his culture, conscious, forever conscious, however, that he had experienced a most traumatic start in this life. Mma Ramotswe identified with Mma Potokwani's philosophy in caring for the children at the Orphan Farm:

'We want to make so many good memories for them that the bad ones are pushed into a corner and forgotten.' (The Good Husband of Zebra Drive)

They told him of the encyclopaedic knowledge of plants and wildlife and remarkable resourcefulness and resilience of his people who had lived in the Bush for thousands of years, a challenging environment in which Mr J.L.B. Matekoni and Mma Ramotswe recognised that most of us wouldn't survive for more than a few days. Water is scarce in the Kalahari and sometimes the precious commodity is found through digging holes or from roots, and empty ostrich eggs are used as flasks.

All around her there was nothing – just endless bush that stretched away to the bounds of the Kalahari on the one side and the plains of the Limpopo on the other. Empty bush, with nothing in it, but some cattle here and there and the occasional creaking windmill bringing up a tiny trickle of water for the thirsty beasts; nothing, nothing, that was what her country was so rich in – emptiness. (The No. 1 Ladies' Detective Agency)

While Mma Ramotswe encouraged Motholeli and Puso to remember that their biological mother loved them, Mma Ramotswe would not herself have chosen their omnivorous diet. She knew that the Bushmen would make ostrich egg omelette by mixing the giant yolk and white with a stick and pouring it direct into hot ash fashioned into a bowl shape. Sometimes the Masarwa, who were remarkable hunters, would have ostrich meat and *duiker* but she was glad to be able to give her step–children regular meals and knew that they appreciated her cooking, in particular Puso, who always cleaned his plate. Puso seemed a natural trapper and Mr Polopetsi, whose own father had taught him to track, encouraged Puso. The Bushmen are also expert hunters and incredibly physically fit, able to run great distances and follow their prey for many miles. Any kind of meat available will be roasted or boiled over an open fire and nothing of the animal will be wasted. While the men do most of the hunting, the women provide the majority of the food, travelling great distances like the men, and returning with nuts, fruits and edible plants.

Chapter 3

Stew and the Comfort of Heavenly Food

Respect for Cattle

They shared the land with cattle and with birds and the many other creatures that could be seen if only one watched. It was easy perhaps not to think about this in the town, where there was food to be had from shops and where running water came from taps, but for many people this was not how life was.

(Morality for Beautiful Girls)

Mma Ramotswe is a true Motswana in her love of and respect for cattle. Her late father Obed Ramotswe, in common with many of his generation, had looked upon his cattle as if they were family and some imagined the ancestors and cattle in heaven. Such was their knowledge of their animals that they could tell one member of a large herd from another, based on a partial sighting at an oblique angle moving at speed in the bush.

It was essential, in Mma Ramotswe's mind, both out of respect for these fine animals and for the taste of the meat, that their end was as swift and dignified as possible.

Meat is the Main Thing

. . . boys should have good appetites, and it was natural for them to want to eat large amounts of cake and sweet things. As they grew older, they would move to meat, which was very important for a man.
(The Kalahari Typing School for Men)

Meat is the main thing and meat, in Botswana, means beef. Yes, there is other meat, but beef is No. 1 by a long way. It is important for strength – that is a well known fact, thought Mma Ramotswe – particularly when cooked on the bone. Batswana like their meat well done and are used to taking time over chewing it. If a meal did not contain meat, many Batswana men would state matter-of-factly that they had not eaten. Any side-salad or 'green stuff' that strays onto the plate of some traditional-minded Batswana men is likely to be treated with some contempt. Protein is much prized and men who can afford it bank on a hefty portion.

. . . perfection was what Botswana wanted for its meat. After all, Botswana beef was fine, grass-fed beef, and tasted so much better than the meat of those poor cattle which were kept cooped up or which were fed food that cattle should not eat.
(In the Company of Cheerful Ladies)

The Botswana Meat Commission (BMC) has extremely high standards and thanks to the far-sightedness of those who took pre-emptive steps to protect Botswana's cattle from major disease, such as Foot and Mouth, is one of the few African countries today allowed to export their quality meat all over the world, indeed it is much sought after. It is true that Botswana imports a great deal from her neighbour, South Africa, but it should be a matter of national pride that this thriving industry, founded on Botswana's excellent cattle, enables people anywhere in the world to experience Botswana's first-class produce. Better still, due to the affluence of the nation, more and more people in Botswana are themselves able to eat the excellent beef, produced in their own country.

An eighth of the income at Tlokweng Road Speedy Motors came from a cattle transport firm owned by a friend of Mr J.L.B. Matekoni's and Mma Ramotswe was sure that this success was due both to efficiency and to the standards of care accorded by this company to the animals. She had once had, from her point of view, a rather unsatisfactory exchange with one of the Apprentices about the last journey of a chicken, tied to the back of a bicycle and this coalesced in her mind with an image of a dung beetle in the vegetable garden in the House of Hope which had struck her emblematically as:

a small bit of nature struggling with another small bit of nature, but as important as everything else in the world
(The Full Cupboard of Life)

Rra Read's Morula Steak

Serves 10 – 12

The Head Chef at the Gaborone Sun Hotel, Rra Read, first enjoyed this memorable dish under a huge old *Morula* tree on a friend's farm in the Tuli block, hence its name. He had given the recipe to Phuti Radiphuti's aunt who was known for her acuity of mind and liked the fact that this is similar to a *braai* (barbecue) dish, but has more to it.

Ingredients:

7 – 8 lbs (2-inch thick) slice of beef buttock, bone in (your butcher will have to prepare this)

Marinade:

Juice from 1 lemon

1 tbs olive oil

Coarse salt

Black pepper (freshly ground)

1 tbs crushed dried chilli

3 cloves crushed garlic

Method:

Mix all marinade ingredients and rub onto the steak, cover and rest for a minimum of 2 hours at room temperature. Flame-grill over hot coals on the *braai* (barbecue), until the 2 sides have a nice grilled colour. Place the steak onto an oven tray and roast it in a 200°C pre-heated oven for 18 minutes if you like it medium rare or longer if you want it well done, as most Batswana do. When you take it out the oven let it rest at room temperature for at least 10 minutes; this will allow the meat to relax and it will become tender.

To serve – slice thin strips off the steak as you would with roast beef, and serve with baked sweet potatoes and a fresh green salad.

Attracting a Fancier Sort of Girl

'You're not eating enough meat! A girl like you needs meat so that she can have lots of children.' (Tears of the Giraffe)

The Apprentices had their own ideas about the fortifying powers of meat and with their wolf-whistling and cat-calling that made ladies feel shy, Mr J.L.B. Matekoni often wondered whether he was making any headway with these two young men. Charlie, the older of the two, who had a chequered relationship with Mma Makutsi, had smirked when he heard that Mma Ramotswe was collecting recipes, and wiping his oily hands on his overalls, string hanging out of his pocket, had shouted to the younger one who was barely six feet away that there should be a recipe for warthog, barbecued at a *braai*. This remark that had fortunately been out of Mma Makutsi's earshot was met with a sharp look from Mma Ramotswe.

'Fast food for fast girls, Oww Mma!' the older Apprentice had later grinned wolfishly. Mma Ramotswe recalled Motholeli's suggestion to Mr J.L.B. Matekoni some time back that he open a 'Tlokweng Road Speedy Restaurant'. He had been typically self-deprecating; she remembered his words: *'I am only good at fixing cars. That is all I can do.'* (The Full Cupboard of Life). While this was not the case by any means, she was somehow relieved that the idea had not been pursued.

Charlie's baiting had no particular season and he had gone on to suggest that on glamorous dates, he and modern girls did not waste too much time eating. It was a good thing that this fast talk and the misguided praise of burgers and hot dogs had been cut short by the return of Mr J.L.B. Matekoni.

Men can forget, however, that ladies talk to one another and Mma Ramotswe knew from Charlie's aunt that he had in fact sought her assistance in a cooking matter. How could he attract a 'fancier sort of girl', as he had put it, with an impressive dish. After a short lecture on looks being only skin deep, the older lady had seized the opportunity to pass on some practical knowledge to her nephew and taught Charlie to make Ostrich Carpaccio and a traditional dish with *tswii*, a potato-like water lily which is common in the Okavango and for which many medicinal claims are made.

Car-patchy-Oww!

Serves 12

A firm supporter of Botswana beef, Mma Ramotswe was not herself enamoured with ostrich (which she thought undignified), but knew many people who were. Some favoured the low cholesterol meat which was said to reduce the incidence of needing a traditionally built cuff to take blood pressure.

Ingredients:

3 lbs beef/ostrich fillet or rump

Fresh herbs — parsley, thyme, chives, basil

Olive oil

Balsamic vinegar

Crushed black pepper

Ground coarse salt

Parmesan cheese

Rocket leaves

Method:

Season the steak with some salt and pepper.

Seal meat in a pan with butter/oil.

Roll meat in the fresh chopped herbs, then roll the beef or ostrich meat tightly in cling film to hold shape.

Freeze overnight or 4 – 5 hrs.

Remove the cling film and slice the meat as thinly as possible. It is important to be on good terms with your butcher and this is an occasion in which it would be helpful if he would slice the meat in his slicing machine.

Allow to defrost.

Serve on platters garnished with the parmesan and rocket leaves and drizzle with olive oil and balsamic vinegar, and sprinkle with salt and pepper to taste.

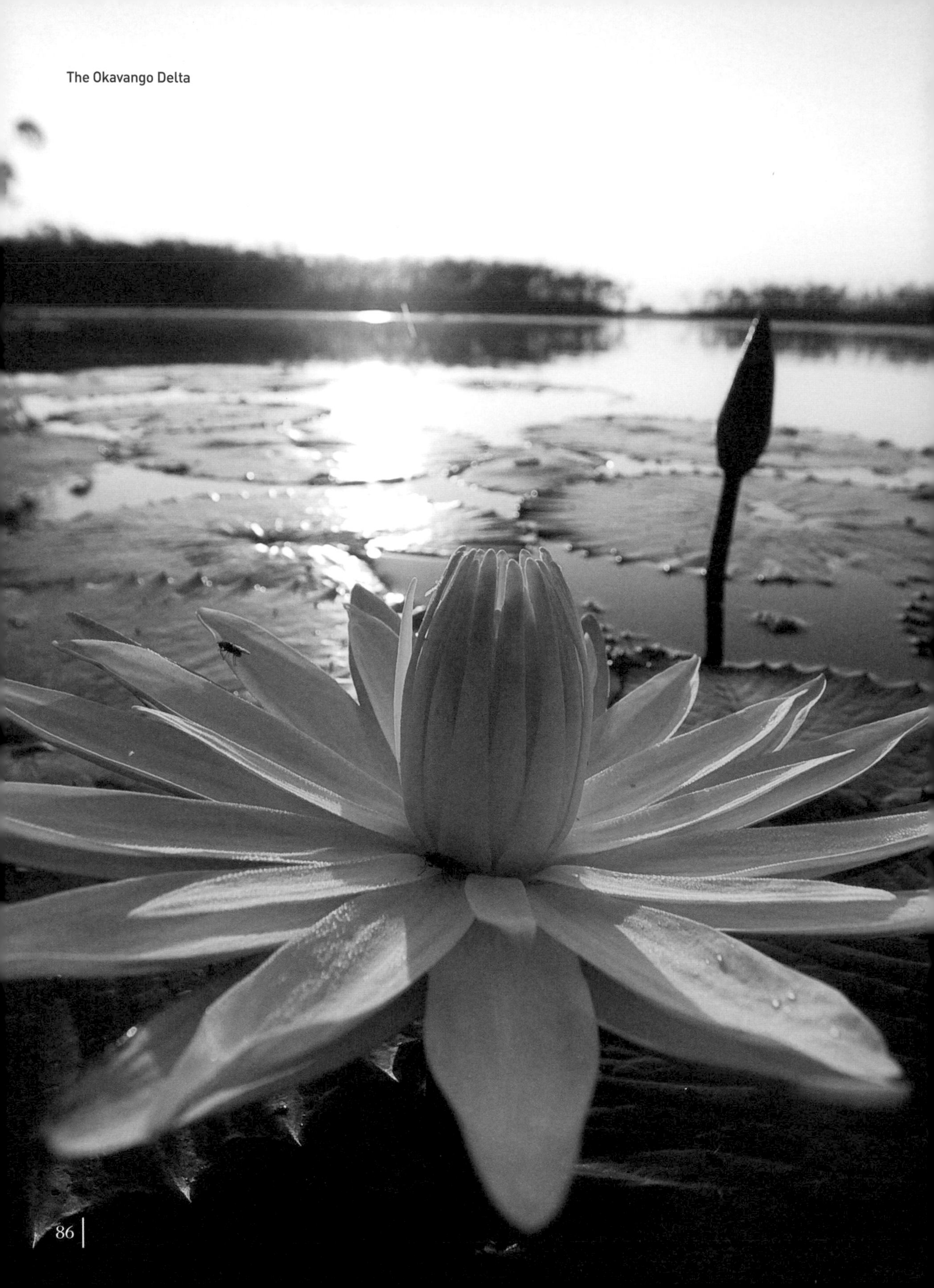

Tswii – Water Lily Potato and Beef (common in Ngamiland district)

Serves 8

Ingredients:

1 cup of shredded and dried *tswii* **(water lily)**	**1 lb 6 oz beef**
¼ cup cooking oil	**2 tsp salt**
1 jug water	

Method:

Put the meat in the pot and place the shredded *tswii* **on top. Pour over a jug of water and leave to cook. Cooking takes 3 hours or more, adding water from time to time. Add a little salt and oil, but do not try to stir as this will burn the food. When ready, the** *tswii* **on top will become soft. Mash the meat until it is soft and thoroughly mixed with the** *tswii***. Serve on its own or with** *phaletshe***.**

She soon found out what Phuti liked to eat, and she made sure that she always cooked these dishes for him. He liked meat, of course, and T-bone steaks in particular, which he would pick up and gnaw at with gusto. He liked marrow and broad green beans doused in melted butter, and he liked chopped-up biltong soaked in gravy and then served over mashed potato. All of these dishes she did for him, and each time he complimented her enthusiastically on her cooking as if it were the first time he had said anything about it. (Blue Shoes and Happiness)

Stew

It is important that a meal is properly filling, stated Mma Ramotswe to herself. Years ago she had heard of a new food movement (that fortunately had not caught on in Botswana) which had prided itself on the smallness of its dishes – the smaller the better apparently. This was very odd indeed and would not do at all in Botswana. The cousin of Fano Fanope, the dance teacher whose classes had brought Mma Makutsi and Phuti Radiphuti together, was a chef who ran his own catering company called Amuse-Bush or some such name. She had seen this man at the newspaper stall outside the Pay-less supermarket, wearing sunglasses on a winter's day when it was really quite overcast. After exciting postings overseas he had returned with international ideas about food and sometimes cooked at one of the embassies in Gaborone. She knew this from one of the traditionally built stallholders in the main mall whose aunt did the dishes there. This aunt, who was herself a traditionally built lady had confirmed Mma Ramotswe's suspicions that many of these international meals would not have nourished the traditionally built frame; not by a long stretch. There was nothing amusing, reflected Mma Ramotswe about meagre portions and she made a mental note to discuss wedding catering with Mma Makutsi who had already begun looking at menus with a lady Phuti knew who had her own refrigerated truck. She was sure that Mma Seconyana, Rose's cousin who was in charge of the kitchens in Mr Bobologo's school and fed 400 mouths every day, would have some good ideas for traditional catering. Mma Ramotswe hoped that not all the wedding food would be spicy. Exotic foreign food didn't always agree with her and she liked regular Setswana dishes such as stews, pumpkin, mealie meal and *seswaa*.

Like its big-hearted people, much of Botswana's food is hearty and its stews are a firm favourite. They are traditionally served with sorghum or mealie meal, but Mma Ramotswe often has potatoes which are also accompanied by samp, rice or bread. So divine is Mma Ramotswe's stew that it forms Mr J.L.B. Matekoni's vision of heaven. Oblivious to Mma Makutsi and Phuti's dance around the issue of feminism, from the comfort of the expensive leather armchair (which before Phuti's double-comfort discount is equivalent to the price of an engine re-bore) Mr J.L.B. Matekoni conjures a picture of paradise:

In the background, in the kitchen, Mma Ramotswe would be preparing the evening meal and the tantalising smell of one of her rich stews would come wafting down the corridor. It was a vision of perfection, a glimpse of what heaven might be like, if one ever got there (Blue Shoes and Happiness)

Stew and the Comfort of Heavenly Food

Zebra Drive Guinea Fowl Stew

Serves 8

Ingredients:

2 Guinea fowl cut into pieces
4 rashers of bacon chopped up
3 chopped onions
2 cloves crushed garlic
1 cup pearl barley
5 cups of chopped-up mixed vegetables such as carrots and green beans
Oil and seasoning

Method:

Brown the guinea fowl pieces and fry the bacon pieces with the onion and garlic in oil. Add the pearl barley and the mixed vegetables and cover with water. Add salt and pepper to taste. Cook on low heat for 2 – 3 hours until the fowl is tender and the stew has thickened. Add some corn flour mixed with a little water to thicken the sauce if necessary.

'It is better for us to be in the kitchen, Mma,' said Mma Tafa. 'I am cooking a stew and I do not want it to spoil. If we sit there, then I can watch it.'

'I like to be in the kitchen,' said Mma Ramotswe. 'It is often the most comfortable room in the house. A sitting room can be too formal, don't you find, Mma?' (The Miracle at Speedy Motors)

Traditional Oxtail Stew

Serves 4

Oxtail is a particular favourite in Botswana. This is a delicious, thick stew ideal for the winter.

Ingredients:

1 medium oxtail cut into pieces
2 onions
1 green pepper
10 – 12 sliced mushrooms
5 sticks of celery
A 16 fl oz jar of pre made beef stock
1 pt of water
4 chopped carrots
3 chopped tomatoes
2 crushed garlic cloves

Method:

Oxtail naturally creates something of a brown scum which needs to be skimmed off regularly as you cook. Alternatively, in advance of cooking, steep the oxtail in a pan of salt water for up to two hours. Replace with fresh water and bring to the boil, skimming the froth off frequently. Leave it to simmer while you have a cup of bush tea. Remove from water and wipe off any residue. Fry oxtail until brown, add the garlic, vegetables and mushrooms and fry for a few minutes more. Cover oxtail pieces with water and add stock. Cook until the oxtail is soft (2 – 3 hours depending on size) and keep on adding water/stock during the cooking process so that it does not cook dry.

Oxtail Stew with Groundnuts

Serves 4

Ingredients:

One cut-up oxtail, about 10 – 12 pieces
9 oz groundnuts (peanuts), skinned and crushed
1 onion, chopped
1 tomato, chopped
1 clove garlic, crushed

Method:

Follow the process described on the previous page to remove the brown film. Boil the oxtail in water in a thick bottomed pot until tender (approximately 2 – 3 hours), keep on adding water as necessary so that sit does not boil dry. In a separate pot, boil 3 cups of water, add the nuts, and cook for 5 minutes. Add onion, tomato and garlic. Add oxtail and its stock and cook for a further 30 minutes.

Mma Tafa's Fragrant Stew

Serves 4

Mma Tafa's brisket stew is quite light, but it is also very fragrant and tasty. This is just as well, thought Mma Ramotswe, since the wife of Big Man Tafa has a laugh that is like an elephant's stomach rumbling and those around her must be constantly thinking about food, not that there is anything wrong with that, she had quickly added to herself. It is delicious when cooked the day before and stored in the fridge.

Ingredients:

2 lbs brisket
3 large potatoes
3 onions, chopped
3 large beef tomatoes, de-skinned and seeded, roughly chopped
1 tsp medium curry powder
1 tsp paprika (smoked paprika if you prefer this)
½ green pepper, finely chopped (not a traditional ingredient but Batswana have become used to them)
1 piece of root ginger, cut into large chunks
1 clove of garlic
1 tbs tomato ketchup
1 tbs tomato paste (optional for extra richness)
1 tbs lemon juice
1 tbs sunflower / vegetable oil
Small amount of chopped fresh coriander for serving

Method:

Trim excess fat off brisket, rinse and cut into 1½ inch pieces.

Lightly season and brown in half the oil in a heavy-bottomed casserole/pan.

Remove meat from pan, reserve juices and skim off any impurities.

Fry chopped onion in remaining oil until soft.

Add the green pepper, spices, garlic, tomato and ketchup and fry until green pepper has softened a little.

Add meat, potato and stir fry for 2 minutes.

Add reserved juices and water to just cover the ingredients and bring to boil. Skim off any impurities, then reduce to a simmer.

Cook, stirring occasionally, for 2 hours 45 minutes (rough guideline: 30 – 40 minutes per 1 lb plus another 30 – 40 minutes).

Garnish with a sprinkling of freshly chopped coriander

Mopane Worms are a delicacy in Botswana

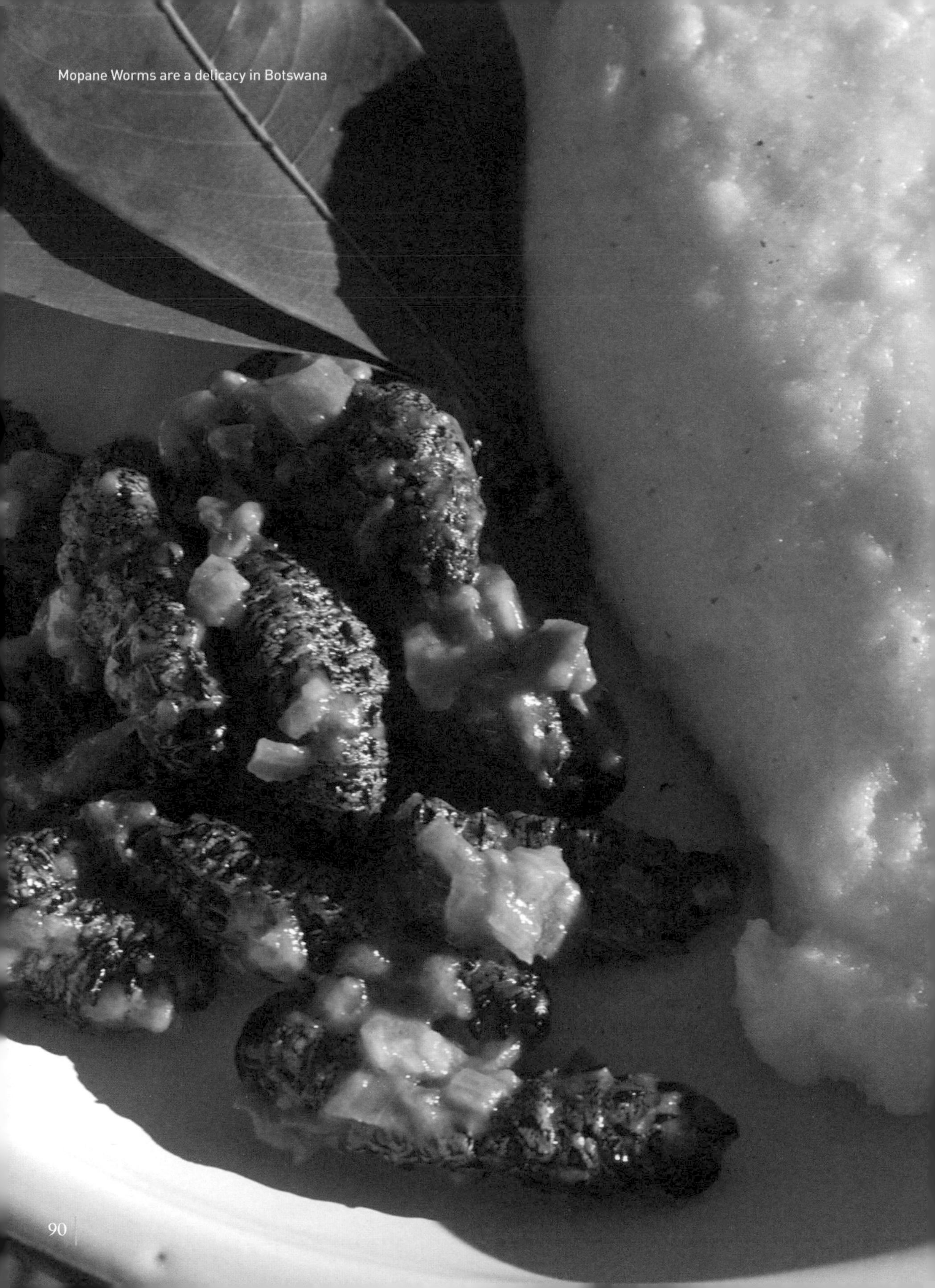

Mma Makutsi made the evening meal with care. She boiled a large pot of potatoes and simmered a thick beef stew into which she put carrots and onions. The stew smelled rich and delicious and she dipped a finger into the pot to taste it. It needed a little bit more salt, but after that it was perfect. (Blue Shoes and Happiness)

Venison Stew

Serves 8

Ingredients:

5 – 6 lbs cubed venison

8 oz white vegetable fat (shortening)

2 tsp thyme

1 tsp garlic salt or 2 crushed cloves garlic

1½ cups diced carrots

2 large onions, chopped

Salt and pepper to taste

Method:

Brown cubed venison in the vegetable fat. Add all ingredients and allow to simmer until meat can be flaked with a fork, 1 – 2 hours.

Mopane Worm Stew

Serves 4

Ingredients:

1½ cups of dried *phane* (*Mopane* worms)

1 tomato, chopped

1 onion, chopped

1 tsp salt

2 tbs oil, butter or margarine

3 tbs peanut butter

Method:

Fry onion in the oil in a saucepan until brown. Add the tomato, salt and *phane* and a little water. Cook the *phane* until soft, add peanut butter and stir until it is well mixed. Cook for 10 minutes and serve hot.

Mopane Worms

Considered a tremendous delicacy in Botswana, as snails are in France, *Mopane* worms are extremely popular and much enjoyed across Southern Africa. *Mopane* worms (*Imbrasia belina*) are caterpillars that mature from the eggs of the beautiful Mopane Emperor Moth.

The insects are voracious eaters and feast principally, but not exclusively, on the leaves of the *Mopane* tree. They are harvested by hand during the summer months. The innards are removed and the worms dried in the open on canvas sheets. This is a precarious source of important income in rural economies in Southern Africa and a valuable source of protein. In market stalls and by the roadside, traditional woven baskets and colourful basins brim with these favourite 'bugs' that are sold dried or smoked. They are also available in cans. Batswana love to eat *Mopane* worms crisp, fried as a tasty snack in place of crisps or beer nuts when the outer skin is peeled off, as one does with prawns. *Mopane* worms are also widely regarded to be delicious in a simple tomato and onion stew.

The cook, Poppy Maope, whom Mma Ramotswe considers to be even more traditionally built than her and who had won the Pick-and-Pay cooking competition, was happy to share her recipe for *Mopane* worms, accepting that people interested in sampling this delicacy could do so when visiting Botswana.

'I was always interested in cooking, Mma. When I was a girl I was always the one in the kitchen, cooking all the food for the family. My grandmother was the one who taught me. She had always cooked and she could make very simple food taste very good. Maize meal. Sorghum. Those very plain things tasted very good when my grandmother had added her herbs to them. Herbs or a little bit of meat if we were lucky, or even chopped up Mopane worms. Oh, those were very good. I cannot resist Mopane worms, Mma? Can You?'

'No Motswana can resist them,' said Mma Ramotswe, smiling. 'I would love to have some right now, but I'm sorry, Mma . . .' (Blue Shoes and Happiness)

Mma Ramotswe had never known her paternal grandfather, Boamogetswe Ramotswe and though he doubtless lived on in Mma Ramotswe in certain features and mannerisms, Boamogetswe's was a generation lost to Mma Ramotswe. Perhaps she took her relish for *Mopane* worms from him. Of course it was a well-known fact that the late Sir Seretse Khama loved *Mopane* worms. She had been discussing this with the Executive Chef at the President Hotel, Amos Mibenge, for whom Poppy's husband worked. Chef Mibenge shared the store she placed in knowing where you have come from and of the importance in passing on knowledge down through the generations. He and his kitchen helpers also cooked excellent Setswana food and where would her Saturdays be without that, thought Mma Ramotswe.

Seswaa: pounded meat is a favourite traditional dish,
often prepared by the men

Roast Leg of Springbok

Serves 8 – 10

Ingredients:

l leg of Springbok or other joint of game meat	**Olive oil**
l dessert spoon plain flour	**Salt, pepper, herbs**

Many people consider the meat of Springbok to be the finest of all wild meats. This recipe works very well for the hind leg of any small to medium sized antelope (or deer, if you live in Europe, New Zealand or North America) or any small to medium sized roasting joint of any antelope. Thinner joints, such as the shoulder, require a little less cooking time. A hind leg of Springbok should weigh 6½ – 12 lb.

Method:

If the joint has been frozen or chilled, thaw completely and bring to room temperature before you start to cook it.

Pour some olive oil into the palm of your hand and then rub it well into the joint. Then sprinkle fine salt all over the joint, with a little freshly ground black pepper and coriander if you like. The purpose of the salt and oil is to form a hard crust on the joint which will keep the juices inside.

Preheat the oven to 230⁰C. Make sure the oven has reached full temperature before you put the meat in. Let the meat start at this high temperature (to seal the juices into the joint) for 10 to 15 minutes. (More for thicker joints, less for thinner.) Then reduce the heat to 190⁰C for the remainder of the cooking time, which is 5 minutes plus 15 minutes per lb. It helps to conserve moisture in the joint if you cover it loosely with a piece of aluminium foil for about half the cooking time after you reduce the heat. Don't overcook it or it will dry out.

Total cooking time for a 11 lb leg will be 20 minutes plus 165 minutes = 3 hours 5 minutes and for a 6½ lb shoulder, 15 minutes plus 99 minutes = 1 hour 54 minutes.

When the joint is cooked, take it out of the oven and put it on a carving dish and cover it for about 20 minutes, a metal meat cover is best but a clean cardboard box does very well if you have nothing else. This will tenderise the meat further. Do not put it in the warming oven, as this will dry it out.

While the meat is resting, prepare the gravy. Since the joint will run no fat, you must use olive oil (or sheep fat). Heat the oil/fat in a saucepan and then add a dessert spoon of plain flour. Cook the flour in the oil and then add some boiling water from cooking vegetables (beans, peas or carrots, not cabbage or other brassicas) and any juices that ran out of the joint, stir to a smooth creamy sauce and simmer for ten minutes. Add a little thyme, sage, rosemary and black pepper to taste.

Seswaa **(Pounded Meat)**

When talking of traditional Botswana dishes, often one of the first to be mentioned is *Seswaa*. This dish of shredded meat is popular with people of all ages. Any meat that does not have too many bones, such as stewing cuts (chuck or brisket) can be used since this is a slow-cooking dish. One day, Mma Ramotswe hopes she will get a slow-cooker after finding the best prices available. The game variety of *Seswaa* is particularly rich. *Seswaa* is regularly made for special occasions such as weddings, funerals and harvest thanksgiving festivals and will often be prepared by the men. Women in Botswana are no strangers to hard physical work, but they will say that the men do the *Seswaa* because of the strength required. *Seswaa* had been one of Obed Ramotswe's favourites and Precious remembered him in his hat, the one from the General Dealer in Mochudi, standing over one of the great big three-legged pots smiling down at her broadly.

Traditional spinach is enjoyed on its own and as an accompaniment to main courses

Venison Seswaa

Serves 4

Ingredients:

2 lb 4 oz stewing venison on the bone
Salt
White pepper

Method:

Arrange the venison in a stewing pot and half fill with water.

Bring to boil and then reduce heat to simmer for 3 hours.

When thoroughly cooked and meat is falling off the bone, remove meat from pot and put the meat in a thick bottomed container and pound until meat separates from sinew. It should have no tendon or bone remaining. Keep the water in the pot.

Season the water with salt and white pepper and mix thoroughly.

Pour the liquid onto the meat and simmer until it reduces.

Serve hot with sorghum meal, samp or mealie meal.

Serobe (Offal)

The late Sir Seretse Khama particularly enjoyed *Serobe*.

Ingredients:

Mixture of tripe and intestines cut into small pieces
Jug of water
1 tbs salt

Method:

Place the mixture in a pot of boiling water and leave to cook. Cooking may take more than 1 hour, depending on quality of meat. Add boiling water from time to time and oil, then salt. Leave to cook. When ready, the mixture will be soft and tasty. Serve with *mosoko* or *ting* on the side.

Bishop Trevor Mwamba who is partial to traditional dishes of Botswana

Mokwetjepe

Serves 12

Mma Ramotswe found that in general, Batswana Men liked these sorts of dishes – anything to do with the insides. Some tripe recipes call for lungs, others don't. This one is from Zambia and a favourite of Bishop Trevor Mwamba, a very learned man, who works to nourish people's insides in a spiritual way and who, Mma Ramotswe was delighted to discover, liked to cook. After uncovering this fact, something of a shibboleth in Mma Ramotswe's value system, she had determined to pay more attention in the cathedral. This recipe includes the spleen which is not the way in Botswana, but for all these recipes you just need to clean properly and boil, boil, boil. The Bishop confided in Mma Ramotswe that he was also particularly partial to *Seswaa, Mopane* worms, Setswana chicken and ginger beer according to the recipe of his mother-in-law, Lady Masire, the wife of the former President, Sir Ketumile Masire. It must be important, thought Mma Ramotswe that bishops understand the passions of their flock and his own tastes in traditional cooking had only increased her good opinion of this man who had united Mr J.L.B. Matekoni and herself in marriage.

Ingredients:

8 oz beef offal
8 oz beef spleen
8 oz beef lungs
8 oz beef intestines
1 oz salt

Method:

Wash the beef ingredients thoroughly, making sure there is no dirt left in them.

Place in a 3-legged pot or stove-top and boil for 4 hours.

Season with the salt.

Using a large pair of strong scissors or shears chop the mixture until fine.

Cook at low heat slowly until the meat blends well with the liquid.

Serve with fresh potato chips, sweet potato chips, *phaphatha* **or** *magwinya*.
This is particularly good as a morning snack that goes well with tea.

Mogodu (Tripe)

Serves 4

Ingredients:

1 lb 12 oz large beef tripe (cleaned thoroughly)
1 oz salt

Method:

Place the tripe in a stew pan.

Add 3½ pints of water.

Place on cooker and bring to the boil.

Reduce the heat and simmer until the offal is tender.

Season with salt and simmer until the liquid reduces.

Serve with samp and beans, or *Ditloo* **beans with peanuts and vegetables.**

Biltong

Biltong is found all over Southern Africa and is a means of preserving meat. Obed Ramotswe's mother had given him biltong which she had made for him to take to the mines. During the Winter the strips of meat dry fast (in 3 or 4 days) and don't go off, which is a risk in the soaring temperatures of Summer. Before attention was rightly paid to preserving endangered species, game was widely thought to make the best biltong in Botswana. Its rich flavour didn't need seasoning.

Method:

Use young lean meat, because excess fat can cause rancidity and will take too long to absorb the salt.

Cut the meat following the grain and cut large pieces of meat in long strips (8 to 10 inches) and about half an inch thick.

Place meat strips in a container and sprinkle salt over every layer. Make sure the thicker pieces are at the bottom since they need more salt. Sprinkle a little vinegar over each layer of meat after it has been salted. Let it sit over night. Next day dip the meat into hot vinegar water (½ pint vinegar to a gallon of boiling water). Hang it under a tree or in a shady place where there is a breeze. Little metal hooks or strong, semi-unfurled paperclips can be used to hang the meat on a string. The process can take several days. Some people like their biltong slightly moist, like a salami, while others prefer it dry. The marinade can be adapted by adding pepper, chilli or garlic. Store biltong in a muslin bag and hang in a draught or slice it and store. Never store biltong in plastic. Biltong can be frozen and thawed at room temperature.

Cooked Biltong (Rehydrated)

Ingredients:

5 pieces of Biltong, cut up into small pieces
1 cup water
2 tbs of butter/margarine
1 onion, chopped
Salt and pepper to taste

Method:

Put the biltong into a saucepan. Cover it with water and bring to the boil. Simmer it on low heat until it is tender. 'Pound' it with a spoon against the edge of the saucepan until it is finely minced. Fry the onions until transparent in the butter and add the meat with a little stock. Season. Serve it hot.

Mochudi Chops

Serves 4

Pork had a place in Mma Ramotswe's affections for several reasons. It has long been popular in Mochudi, and was among the favourite dishes of the excellent Sir Seretse Khama.

Ingredients:

1 lb pork chops
3 tbs tomato sauce
½ tsp mustard
Salt

3 tbs vinegar
3 tbs Worcester sauce
1 finely chopped onion

Method:

Sprinkle chops with salt and lay them in a sauce made from the other ingredients, mixed well. After half an hour fry chops in a little fat. Heat the sauce separately and pour over chops to serve.

Makutsi Curry

Serves approximately 6 people

Ingredients:

4 medium oxtails

1 large onion (peeled and chopped)

5 or 6 garlic cloves *(alternatively you can use approx 1 to 1½ tsp of pre-mixed crushed/paste garlic and ginger)*

Fresh root ginger

Salt

Fresh coriander

1 tsp mixed masala

3 or 4 medium tomatoes (peeled and grated or chopped)

4 medium potatoes (peeled and cut into 4 pieces)

Sunflower/vegetable oil

White pepper

¾ tsp roasted masala

1 tsp cumin powder

Method:

Crush garlic and ginger together (add a pinch of salt).

Cut oxtail into pieces on joints or smaller.

Cut off excess fat.

Cover with water in large saucepan, and boil until tender (approx 1 hour).

Once tender transfer meat and broth to another container.

Using same saucepan brown onions, garlic and ginger.

Add spices and meat and sauté for a short while before adding tomatoes.

Allow a few minutes for spices to cook through before adding potatoes.

Using a wooden spoon stir lightly to ensure spices are well mixed.

Add salt and white pepper to taste.

On medium heat allow to cook until potatoes are ready, adding water and/or left over broth when required.

Once cooked, sprinkle chopped coriander over the oxtail dish and mix just before serving. Serve with rice.

Dr Moffat's Beef Madras

Serves 8

Ingredients:

1 cup grated fresh coconut

2 tbs grated fresh ginger

1 tbs tamarind concentrate

2 large onions, sliced

1 tsp ground cumin

2 tsp ground coriander

2 tsp sweet paprika

2lb 4 oz diced beef chuck steak

6 oz can tomatoes

2 tsp black mustard seeds

2 tbs vegetable oil

6 cloves garlic, crushed

1 tsp ground turmeric

2 tsp hot chilli powder

10 curry leaves

½ cup water

Method:

Blend or process coconut, tomatoes, ginger, seeds and tamarind until puréed. Heat the oil in a large saucepan, cook onions and garlic, until brown. Add all the spices and cook until fragrant. Add curry leaves, beef, water and coconut mixture; simmer covered 1½ hours or until beef is tender, stirring every now and then.

Goat/Mutton Curry

Ingredients:

About 2 lb of Goat or Sheep on the bone

1 large or 2 medium onions

1 large or 2 medium green peppers

1 large or 2 medium tomatoes

1 mango or apple

2 – 3 cloves garlic

3 – 5 thin slices of fresh root ginger

Sheep fat or cooking oil

About 1 tsp each of turmeric, coriander, cumin and whole black pepper corns

About ½ tsp each of cinnamon bark, star anise or fennel seeds, and fenugreek

2 – 3 whole cloves

2 – 3 cardamom pods

Salt and chilli to taste

Method:

Cut the meat into bite-sized pieces and put aside in a dish.

Take the coriander, cumin, whole black pepper corns, cinnamon bark, anise (or fennel seeds), fenugreek, whole cloves, cardamom pods and chilli and grind them together finely. Add the turmeric and mix it in well. Mix well together with the meat, until it is evenly coated. Put aside.

Slice the onion(s) and start to fry them in a suitable pot. Then cut up the green pepper(s) and add to the onions when they are soft. Continue to fry until the onions start to caramelise (brown) and the green peppers are soft. Put aside.

Now fry the meat in the same pot (you will need to add extra oil or fat).

When the meat is just done, add the onions and peppers and then cut up the tomatoes and mango (or apple) and add them too. If absolutely necessary (avoid if possible), add a small quantity (not more than ½ cup) of water.

Turn up the heat and bring to a fierce boil quickly. Then turn the heat right down, as low as it will go, so the pot is just simmering very gently and cook for at least 1 hour for sheep or 1½ hours for goat, which is tougher.

In Pursuit of Chicken

Mochudi had a number of restaurants, most of them very small affairs, one small room at the most, or a rickety bench outside a lean-to shack serving braised maize cobs and plates of pap; simple fare, but filling and delicious . . . There was one good restaurant, though, one that she liked, which had a garden and tables in that garden. The kitchens were clean, the food wholesome, and the waitresses adept at friendly conversation. She went there from time to time when she felt that she needed to catch up on Mochudi news, and she would spin out her lunch to two or three hours, talking or just sitting under one of the trees and looking up at the birds on the branches above.

(The Good Husband of Zebra Drive)

Mma Ramotswe had been surprised when, sitting in Mochudi's fine restaurant on the Sikwane road, a steaming plate of stew, samp and pumpkin in front of her, she'd observed a lady in a red dress rush past the entrance pursuing a chicken. A commonplace occurrence, this event was not the source of surprise, but the realisation that she was at that moment being observed by a visitor at another table, a distinguished-looking man with a broadly-brimmed hat. He was evidently a fellow observer of small happenings and Mma Ramotswe wondered if he too was perhaps a Detective in his own country.

Setswana chicken with melon porridge and spinach

Koko ya Setswana (Setswana Chicken)

Serves 8

Chicken in Botswana range freely, as should be the case. Their meat is succulent and flavoursome and more chewy than chicken in Europe and America. In villages, a chicken is killed, swiftly. The whole bird, feathers and all, is put in a pot of boiling water for around twenty seconds to make it easier to pluck. Once plucked, nothing is wasted as all parts of the chicken are cooked for around thirty minutes. The Batswana particularly relish the feet which are cooked with the intestines and head.

Ingredients:

1 whole Setswana chicken

Water

1 tsp hot red peri-peri pepper (cayenne pepper can substitute)

Salt

Method:

Cut into desired size pieces. Put in 3-legged pot over open fire.

Pour 2 coffee mugs full of water into pot.

When it starts boiling add 1 tsp salt.

Stir the chicken before adding a second amount of water.

Keep the pot boiling with additional firewood so that the water may dry up quickly.

Put 2 more coffee mugs full of water into pot. Increase the firewood so that the water dries quickly.

Add the hot red peri-peri pepper for more flavour. It is quite spicy.

Leave a small amount of water as a gravy.

Dish the tender chicken.

It is good served with *phaletshe* or *bogobe*.

She knew what Mma Makutsi's favourites were, and she would make sure these were on the menu. Mma Makutsi liked chicken, especially if it was smothered in garlic, and she enjoyed ice cream served with tinned South African pears. Mma Ramotswe did not particularly like either of these – certainly she avoided garlic and she found that the slightly grainy texture of pears set her teeth on edge. But she would provide both for Mma Makutsi's sake.

(Tea Time for the Traditionally Built)

Dumplinys

Chicken with Dumplings

Serves 8 – 10

Ingredients:

Whole jointed chicken or 10 pieces of raw chicken, on the bone and with skin (thighs, drumsticks, etc.)

1 cup olive oil / cooking oil

½ cup cider or white wine vinegar

1 large clove garlic, finely chopped

1 tbs butter

For the dumplings and sauce

2 pints milk	1 onion, finely chopped
Bunch of finely chopped parsley	2 cups flour
4 tbs unsalted butter (room temperature)	2 tsp baking powder
1 tsp salt	up to 1 cup milk
1 tbs flour	A grating of nutmeg
1 tbs sherry	

Method:

Chicken

The night before, joint and clean chicken and place chicken pieces / joints in a large mixing bowl with the chopped garlic clove. Pour over the vinegar, oil and mix pieces to ensure they are evenly coated. Cover, and refrigerate.

Prior to cooking, preheat oven to 220°C. Line a roasting tin or baking dish with heavy aluminium foil, so that it is wide enough to overlap across the top. Carefully place chicken pieces into the foil covered dish, fitting them in tightly and pouring all oil and vinegar inside the foil, dot with butter and seal the foil, making seal as airtight as possible. Cook for about 40 minutes, until the meat is thoroughly cooked, brown and tender. Transfer the pieces to a casserole dish and keep warm. Set aside the baking dish with juices for later.

Dumplings

About 15 minutes before the chicken has finished cooking, sift flour, salt, baking powder into a mixing bowl. Cut up the butter and then use fingertips to rub in, until the mixture resembles breadcrumbs. Stir in half each of the chopped onions and parsley. Making a well, add half a cup of milk and stir in, then adding a little at a time just until the mixture forms a dry-ish dough.

Bring the 2 pints of milk to nearly boiling, and then drop dumplings, using two teaspoons to pick up and scrape off into the milk. Lower heat to a simmer and cook dumplings for 15 minutes. Remove them with a slotted spoon, placing on top of the chicken pieces in the casserole dish.

Sauce

Place the original baking dish onto the stove top on medium heat. Stir in 1 tbsp flour, mix thoroughly and add enough of the milk in which the dumplings were boiled to make a sauce. The remaining finely chopped onion and parsley improve the sauce and add a grating of nutmeg and tablespoon of sherry at the last minute. Pour sauce over the chicken and dumplings and serve.

Mma Makutsi knew what Phuti Radiphuti's culinary tastes were and had recently discovered that he was particularly partial to peri-peri chicken, a dish that the Portuguese had dreamed up in Mozambique and Angola. From there it had spread into other countries, including Botswana, where it was a favourite amongst those who liked their food to be searingly hot. Phuti was one of these, she thought, and could happily chew on the most stinging of chilli peppers without the need of a glass of water.

'You'll get used to it, Grace,' he said. 'You will not feel it at all. Peri-peri chicken, vindaloo curries – everything. It will all taste equally good.'

She was doubtful, but for Phuti's sake was still prepared to put up with what she thought to be excessively fiery dishes; and now she was making one of these, dropping several large pinches of flaked chilli into the marinade of oil and lemon juice that she had prepared shortly before Phuti's arrival.

(The Miracle at Speedy Motors)

Food is important to Phuti Radiphuti, and whilst for some, *variety* may be the spice of life, for Phuti, a creature of habit who dined in strict rotation with relatives, *spice* was the spice of life, as he liked his food hot. On the shop-floor, Phuti's system of semaphore seemed to convey his intentions to staff so clearly, yet in matters of the heart and particularly in wedding planning with its apparently sensitive topics such as 'bride-price', the wrong words just seemed to tumble out. Mma Makutsi's ability to cook peri-peri chicken and other dishes had been a genuine bonus he'd only discovered *after* having proposed to her, but relationships, as with dancing, seemed to offer such opportunities to put one's foot in it. Having sought counsel in a self-assertiveness manual, Phuti had tried to picture himself surfing the wave of feminism that he feared would sweep him aside. Fortunately, mutual respect and the arrival of pineapple and custard had helped resolve the misunderstanding.

Peri-Peri Chicken

Serves 4

Ingredients:

1 small chicken (cut and separated into legs, wings and breast)/2 lb 4 oz of chicken pieces

Juice of 1 lemon

Juice of 1 lime

2 cloves of garlic, crushed

4 tbs olive/vegetable oil

6 – 10 fresh red chillies, chopped and deseeded

1 heaped tsp salt

1 tsp black pepper, ground

Method:

Combine all ingredients (except the chicken) in a bowl and mix to form a paste.

Pour sauce over the chicken pieces. Marinate in the fridge for a few hours or overnight (the longer the better).

Pre-heat the oven to 180°C – fan-assisted oven 160°C – and oven cook for 45 minutes.

Serve with rice.

Chicken vindaloo

Chicken Vindaloo Devtani

Serves 8

Originating from one of Phuti Radiphuti's cousins, a kindly chef who uses his cooking prowess to see the world, this curry is very hot and spicy, just the way Phuti likes it. This dish is even better the second day.

Ingredients:

2 tsp cumin seeds

2 tsp garam masala

1 tbs grated fresh ginger

6 cloves garlic, crushed

8 small red chillies, chopped finely

1 tbs white wine vinegar

1 tbs tamarind concentrate

2 lb chicken breasts, diced

2 tbs ghee

2 large onions, chopped

2 cinnamon sticks

6 cloves

2 tsp plain flour

1¾ pints chicken stock

8 curry leaves

Method:

Cook cumin and garam masala in large dry saucepan, stirring until fragrant.

Combine cooled spice mixture with ginger, garlic, chillies, vinegar and tamarind in a large bowl, add chicken and mix to coat chicken in marinade. Cover and refrigerate for 1 hour.

Heat ghee in the same pan; cook onion, cinnamon and cloves, stirring till onions are slightly brown.

Add chicken mixture; cook for 5 minutes while stirring until chicken is brown, then stir in the flour.

Gradually pour in stock, add leaves; simmer covered for 20 minutes.

Remove cover and simmer for further 15 minutes or until the sauce has thickened.

Serve with steamed Basmati rice.

The Okavango Delta, navigated by traditional boats: *Mokoro* (opposite)

Fish

There are said to be 85 species of freshwater fish in Botswana but these are confined to the rivers and wetlands of the Okavango Delta in the North (a branch of the Zambezi river) and Botswana's dams (reservoirs). Fishing is a popular weekend activity, often enjoyed as a family from rowing boats or more commonly from the bank or the vantage point of a rock.

Demand for fresh fish has exceeded the local capacity to supply, but in arid areas of this land-locked country, many Batswana will not have any dealings with fish. The Okavango Delta is home to species including the Tiger Fish, an exciting, fast-moving fresh-water fish that will leap four feet in the air, putting up a fight when on the multi-headed *Rapala* lure and which has many bones; *Nembwe* is a large Bream (Tilapia, as widely known in sub-Saharan Africa) with its three round spots, that is delicious when enticed out of hiding in the reeds, cooked and eaten with mealie meal. The whiskered Cat Fish or Barbel is often to be seen for sale near the Gaborone Dam. All of these fish are most commonly boiled, fried, smoked, or sun-dried. A favourite method of cooking is to boil the fish in a large three-legged pot over a fire, with just a little salt.

Richard's Tiger Fish

Serves 6 – 8

Ingredients:

About 1 lb of Tiger fish or other strong flavoured white fish
Up to 1 lb of shell fish (if available, otherwise use more white fish)
1 large or 2 medium onions
1 large or 2 medium green peppers
2 – 3 cloves garlic
3 – 5 thin slices of fresh root ginger
2 cups white rice
Cooking oil
About 1 tsp each of turmeric, coriander, cumin, whole black peppercorns
About ½ tsp cinnamon bark and star anise or fennel seeds
2 – 3 whole cloves
2 – 3 cardamom pods
Salt and chilli to taste
Cold water

Method:

Remove all the bones – Tiger fish have lateral bones as well as the usual vertical ones.

Wash the rice thoroughly in several waters and put aside.

Take the coriander, cumin, whole black peppercorns, cinnamon bark, anise (or fennel seeds), whole cloves, cardamom pods and chilli and grind them together finely. Add the turmeric, garlic and ginger, and mix it in well. Put aside.

Slice the onions and start to fry them in a suitable pot. Then cut up the green peppers and add to the onions when they are soft. Continue to fry until the onions start to caramelise (brown) and the green peppers are soft. Put aside.

Now fry the fish and shellfish until just done. If you have prawns, try to scorch them slightly. Just before they are done, add the spice mixture, stir it in and fry for two minutes or so until fish is done. Now add the onions and peppers, stir well, then add the rice, stir more and then add 2¼ cups of cold water, add salt to taste. Turn the heat full up and bring to the boil quickly. When the pot is boiling vigorously, turn the heat right down, as low as it will go, so the pot is just simmering very gently. Leave for about 20 minutes until all water is absorbed and the rice just cooked. Turn off the heat and let stand for a further 5 minutes of so and then dish up.

Bream on the Braai

Ingredients:

Bream
Butter
Garlic salt
Black pepper

Method:

Fillet the bream and place each fillet in tin foil with 1 tbs butter, a sprinkle of garlic salt and a little black pepper. Seal the tinfoil well so that the butter does not escape.

Cook on a grid over an open fire for approximately 10 minutes. Serve with baked potatoes (also done in their jackets on the fire) and a green salad.

Bream Chowder

Serves 8

Ingredients:

4 lb bream
3 pints water
2 onions
2 carrots
1 stick celery (or tin of mushrooms)
2 small potatoes
1 small green pepper
2 tomatoes
1 clove garlic
1 bay leaf
4 oz butter
2 tbs dry sherry (optional)
½ cup cream (fresh or tinned)
1 tsp flour
salt and pepper

Method:

Skin and fillet the fish. Make stock by boiling skin, bones and head for an hour in water. Strain.

Meanwhile chop all the vegetables into small pieces and fry lightly with chopped garlic and bay leaf in butter.

Stir in fish stock and simmer for 1½ hours over a low heat. Cut fish into small dice and add to vegetables, simmering for a further 15 minutes. Mix flour with sherry (or water), stir into soup and season with salt and pepper to taste. Stir in cream when ready to serve.

Violet Sepotho Tail

Serves 4 – 6

Wild crocodile is protected in Botswana and cannot be hunted or killed without a permit; however, it is farmed there and the meat sold locally as well as being exported. A fairly recent recipe of Mma Makutsi's, this Crocodile tail was one that she liked to give to Phuti Radiphuti. She said that the creaminess provided a cooling contrast to some of the spicy main courses that he so enjoyed. She also muttered in low tones that it was nice for a change when a predator with her big flashy false smile, a reptile so well camouflaged and ready to pounce, got her come-uppance, although this was a remark which passed Phuti by. She remembered Mma Ramotswe telling her that didn't like having to shoot a crocodile herself once, but there it was – some swallowed watches, others like Violet Sepotho, Mma Makutsi's arch-nemesis, might be a husband-stealer . . .

Ingredients:

1 lb of crocodile tail, sliced

1 cup plain flour (for coating)

2 oz butter

1 cup white wine

¾ fresh cream

2 diced tomatoes (only the flesh, not the seeds)

1 diced onion

Salt

Lemon pepper

Fresh parsley

Method:

Season the Crocodile with salt and pepper and death roll it in plain flour. Pan-fry the crocodile tail and onion in butter until browned. Remove the crocodile from pan and de-glaze pan with the white wine; simmer for a few minutes until the liquid has reduced by half, then add the cream and fresh parsley and simmer the sauce until it is reduced by a third. If you need to thicken sauce you can use a little corn-flour mixed with water. Finally return the crocodile to the sauce and stir in the diced tomato at the end. Put your crocodile on a serving plate and pour over the sauce. Garnish with lemon wedges and fresh parsley.

Food was of significance to Phuti, he knew that about himself but wondered which man didn't see eating as important. He had shared his enlightening philosophy on this subject with Violet Sepotho when he told her:

'Good cooking makes people happy . . . And it makes them full.'

(The Miracle at Speedy Motors)

Chapter 4

Dessert: The Stoep in Mochudi

How can one generalise, but Botswana is a nation of well-mannered people and there it is. *Botho* is the observance of respect and manners and the proper way of doing things, which is valued in Botswana. The Setswana greeting for a lady, 'Dumela Mma' and a man, 'Dumela Rra' and asking how they are and if they have slept well is essential and a gesture that is hugely appreciated when welcome visitors to Botswana make this small effort. The correct way of calling out 'Ko ko' and waiting to be invited in, before entering someone's property must be observed.

In Setswana culture, one gives and receives with two hands and thanks can be communicated with a simple yes – 'Eh Mma' or 'Eh Rra' – and – importantly, a smile which can mean so much more than the mechanical formulation of words. Mugs of water are offered in the country and no one hesitates to ask for or to give water. Objects are proffered and received with two hands or with one hand clasping or touching the other arm that is doing the receiving. In the villages, when anything is passed to the Chief or Subordinate Chief, it is done so with a curtsey. A polite guest will eat whatever the host puts on the table for them. *Botho* is also demonstrated at mealtimes in women bringing hot water to all diners for them to wash their hands before eating.

There was no doubt in Mma Ramotswe's mind that Botswana had to get back to the values which had always sustained the country and which had made it by far the best country in Africa. There were many of these values, including respect for age – for the grandmothers who knew so much and had seen so much hardship – and respect for those who were traditionally built . . . (In the Company of Cheerful Ladies)

Kgotla – traditional court in which everyone has a say

A Recipe for Selfishness: Ignoring the Old Botswana Ways

. . . where would we be in a world without the old Botswana morality? It would not work, in Mma Ramotswe's view, because it would mean that people could do as they wished without regard for what others thought. That would be a recipe for selfishness, a recipe as clear as if it were written out in a cookery book: take one country, with all that the country means, with its kind people, and their smiles, and their habit of helping one another; ignore all this; shake about; add modern ideas; bake until ruined. (Blue Shoes and Happiness)

Kgotla

A *Kgotla* is a traditional public gathering, presided over by the village Chief in which decisions affecting a community are reached by consensus. As in many other parts of Africa, the process of *discussion* is greatly valued in Botswana and everyone, irrespective of status, can have their say in the *Kgotla*. Encircled by a distinctive fence of twisted tree branches, this forum can consider any issue of import to the village, including disputes between neighbours and applications for planning permission. The *Kgotla* operates as a court with legal powers to administer punishments of up to five years in prison. The serious punishments administered for the neglect or theft of animals, reflect the importance of livestock in Botswana.

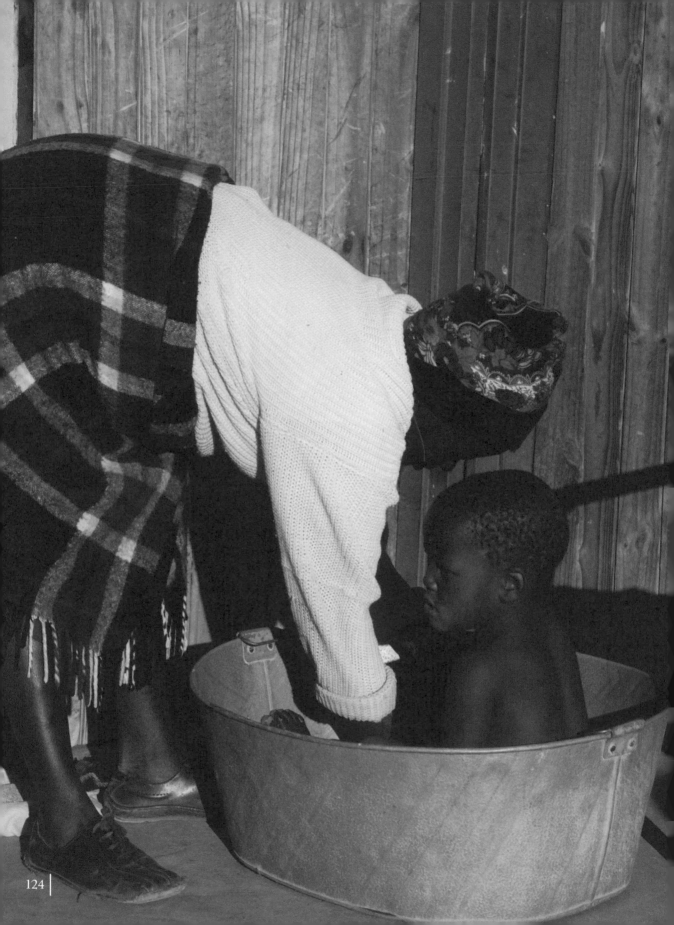

The Importance of Grandmothers

Some of the older people say that things are not quite what they were and their knowledge should be respected, but the same wise commentators light up when visitors share their own honest impressions of Batswana as a strikingly hospitable and friendly people. Impressively, these older Batswana do not think their years afford them exemption from good manners, even if teasing younger ones is their prerogative. Mma Ramotswe knows from her own experience and from the accounts of others that some visitors are touched by the gentle and patient courtesy that they experience in Botswana and she feels proud of this. Movingly content, some smiles or seemingly incidental gestures of warmth and welcome remain in visitors' memories, long after cameras have vanished from suitcases passing through Johannesburg airport and elsewhere.

It was particularly hard for women now, when there were so many children left without parents because of this cruel sickness. These children had to be looked after by somebody, and this task usually fell to the grandmothers. But in many cases the grandmothers were finding it difficult to cope because there were simply so many children coming to them. Mma Ramotswe had met one woman who had been looking after twelve grandchildren, all orphaned. And there this woman was at seventy-five, at a time when a person should be allowed to sit in the sun and look up at the sky, cooking and washing and scraping around for food for the hungry mouths of all those children. And if that grandmother should become late, she thought, what then?

(Blue Shoes and Happiness)

The 'cruel sickness' referred to is, of course, AIDS. The AIDS epidemic which has affected so many parts of Africa has meant that many children face terrible realities that no one should have to and which they often encounter far, far too young. Free drugs are now being provided. Specially-prepared food baskets designed by experts for sick people who need help in getting the right nutrients and enough protein are freely provided by the state. Such is the generosity of people in Botswana that the sick will often share their baskets with members of their family and friends. In turn, as Mma Makutsi nursed her brother Richard with soup, biltong and other tokens of love, those who are well provide whatever they can for their family and friends to offer some moments of salve. Grandmothers, thought Mma Ramotswe, are a precious commodity and people in Botswana have a remarkable resilience and wealth of reserves, much deeper than her diamonds.

The Best Jam in Botswana

Mma Ramotswe examined the jam which Mma Boko was making, and took the small spoonful which her friend offered her.

'This is the best jam in Botswana, I think.'

Mma Boko shook her head. 'There are ladies here in Molepolole who make much better jam than this. I will bring you some jam one day, and you will see.'

'I cannot believe it will be better,' said Mma Ramotswe licking the spoon clean.

(The Kalahari Typing School for Men)

The great jam makers were generally Grandmothers, Mma Ramotswe had found. Mma Makutsi knew that in the ancient martial arts, different levels of skill and mastery were recognised with a particular colour of belt and that a black belt signified the most accomplished category. Jam makers should, she thought be recognised with some similar emblem of distinction, a framed certificate for the kitchen wall or perhaps a *Morula* fruit medal that would be worn on special days that everyone remembered such as Botswana Independence Day and the Birthday of Seretse Khama, or that could be flashed to silence glamorous girls. She had put this to Mma Ramotswe one morning after making two kinds of tea and before the day's business had begun in earnest.

Mr Polopetsi who had been at the 'interagency' kettle at that moment had volunteered that such ladies could become members of the Order of Pectin and put OP after their name as Mma Makutsi used post-nominals to indicate her secretarial qualification. Mma Makutsi's tone in ending any further uninvited contribution reminded Mma Ramotswe of one of Mochudi's more challenging marmalades. At that moment, Mma Ramotswe had herself been reflecting upon the false economy of buying cheap jam, which as with paint, one regrets.

Mma Ramotswe recalled Mr J.L.B. Matekoni telling her that for all their bravado a group of men going into the Bush quickly fall into line with an unspoken understanding of who has the skills needed there and who really are the 'Big Men'. It is the same when it comes to the giants of jam; everyone who counted in the jam world just knew who was big, they really did. Molepolole was jam 'Mecca'. Mma Ramotswe's old friend, Mma Ntombi Boko who had retired there at 54 to run the local branch of the Botswana Rural Women's Association was one such expert. Under that canvas awning porch, in a small brick oven and in a blackened saucepan much award-winning jam had been produced and around it, 'news' exchanged and the world put to rights.

In common with many of the men of his generation who went off to the mines, Obed Ramotswe often travelled with bread and jam sandwiches, presumably, it had occurred to Mma Ramotswe as an adult, for the energy. Mma Ramotswe was herself partial to a sandwich with corned beef or egg but appreciated a good jam nonetheless.

Three Fruit Marmalade

Ingredients:

4 oranges
2 grapefruit
Water
Sugar
3 lemons
1 level tsp of bicarbonate of soda

Method:

Wash and dry fruit, removing stalk ends. Cut into halves and extract juice. Put juice into a bowl and remove pips. Mince fruit, add juice. Measure the fruit using a cup and for each cup allow three cups of water. Leave fruit in the water and juice overnight. Next day boil for 1 hour. Leave overnight again. Add the soda and boil again until rinds are soft. Remove from pan and weigh the fruit and water together. Allow a pound of sugar for every pound of this. Bring fruit and water to the boil then add the sugar, stirring continuously until the sugar has dissolved. Boil fairly fast, stirring often until the jellying stage is reached. Remove and bottle.

Morula Jelly

Ingredients:

Use slightly ripe fruit
1tsb ground ginger (optional)

Method:

Wash *morulas*. With a sharp knife slit skins around the circumference. Add just enough water to cover fruit and boil in a large pot until the skins fall off – about one hour. Strain the juice through muslin, letting it drip through slowly – it can be left over-night. Do not force through the muslin or the jelly will be cloudy. Boil this juice again and do a pectin test.

Test: Pour 1 tbs methylated spirits into a cup; add 1 tsp cooked *morula* juice which should jell if there is sufficient pectin. If not, boil the juice longer.

Add 1 cup sugar for each cup of juice and boil again (adding the ginger if you wish) until the setting stage is reached, at which the jelly falls off a wooden spoon in a sort of curtain and the colour is a clear golden glow. Store in jam jars.

Jam, Beauty and Intoxicated Elephants

During the short harvest period of February and March, Botswana's abundance of *Morula* fruit is harvested. The fruit must be allowed to ripen on the ground for three or four days after it has fallen. Yeast-laden, if left for too long *Morula* can begin to ferment and animals, including elephants, have been known to become rather intoxicated after feasting on this dizzying spread. A swaying elephant emerging from this naturally-occurring bush shebeen or drinking den is best given a very wide berth indeed.

Half of the weight of the *Morula* fruit is in the large seed it contains and this nut is highly prized for its precious oils with Beauty people all over the world interested in tapping into its properties as a product for skins of every colour.

Melons

Melons and watermelons are appreciated with great enthusiasm in Botswana and are a key component in farming and cultivation there. The local variety of melon, the *lekatane*, *lerotse* or traditional Setswana melon is a favourite. The juicy watermelon survives drought that other crops cannot weather, is thirst-quenching and is said to help cleanse the system and enhance one's complexion. The Tsamma Melon or wild watermelon abounds in the Kalahari and is the original ancestor of the watermelon. Variegated, dark green with light green mottled stripes, its hard white flesh can be eaten raw, but is slightly bitter and is more often used in cooking and, with its high pectin content, for making preserves. Its protein-rich seeds are often roasted and enjoyed as a nourishing, traditional snack. The oils from these seeds are also highly prized by the cosmetics industry for their moisturising and restorative properties.

Lekatane (Melon) Jam

Ingredients:

2 cups cooked, mashed *lekatane* **(Setswana melon)**
2 cups sugar
¼ tsp ginger
Juice and rind of 1 large lemon

Method:

Add ginger, lemon juice and lemon rind to the mashed *lekatane*.

Put to boil, and stir in the sugar.

Let it boil rapidly for 15 minutes. Reduce the heat and simmer until it becomes thick, stirring constantly.

Bottle the jam, seal and store till required.

Mulberry Jelly

Method:

Wash 2 lb mulberries and put into an enamel preserving pan or saucepan with just sufficient water to cover. Stew until fruit is tender and water gluey. Strain through sieve.

Weigh the juice and to every 1 lb juice add ¾ lb sugar. Add juice of 1 lemon and boil until it gels.

Pack in dry, sterilized bottles with airtight lids.

Dessert: The Stoep in Mochudi

Being Best: Rest and Tinned Peaches

Mma Ramotswe liked to lie down for twenty minutes or so after the midday meal. On occasions she would drop off to sleep for a short while, but usually she just read the newspaper or a magazine. (Blue Shoes and Happiness)

With all that is on the minds of busy ladies, it is entirely understandable that one occasionally forgets to shop for the family meal. In such situations, particularly on hot days, when lacking energy, one is faced with the dilemma of whether to take a much needed and well deserved nap in the cool of the house or to struggle out to the shops. Even if this journey is not in the peril of the Bush at nightfall, when one is vulnerable to a lion ready for a traditionally built meal, a traditionally built lady should take care of over-exerting herself needlessly. Mma Ramotswe has also recognised that the traditional build can impact upon walking speed.

Your family is not best served by you exhausting yourself when the ingredients for an entirely acceptable meal may be found within the cupboards and a dish rustled up.

With all ladies who pride themselves on being No. 1 for their families, this can be a source of internal struggle. However, a weight can be taken off the mind by taking the weight off one's feet, particularly when the feet in question are traditionally built. Mma Ramotswe had heard this sort of thing talked of in terms of giving oneself 'permission'. Granting oneself the right to provide a tin of peaches in syrup, rather than going to the lengths of producing custard and semolina pudding once in a while, to be properly rested, is a healthy option. This also obviates the risk of an air of martyrdom descending when one can sound rather peevish and resentful about the heroic efforts to which one has gone to provide the best meal possible. It is better instead to go with the inclination to rest with a pot of bush tea and emerge refreshed, a gracious and cheerful provider.

. . . had she bought groceries, she would not be experiencing that extraordinary feeling of renewal that an exciting purchase can bring. And did she really need groceries? There were some potatoes at home, and some spinach. There were also a couple of eggs and some bread. With a little ingenuity, what food there was could be combined to produce a tasty enough morsel for Phuti Radiphuti's dinner – a potato and spinach omelette perhaps, or fried egg and chips, a simple meal, but one which was exactly the sort of thing that men liked to eat. (The Miracle at Speedy Motors)

It is a matter of personal choice whether, when it comes to a stand-off, shoes or groceries are the priority purchase. Mma Makutsi has been known to vote with her feet on this issue, leading to a simple meal that caused her fiancé, Phuti Radiphuti to ask whether a main course was to follow.

One should always make a meal that ends with a pudding. Pudding, in Mma Ramotswe's mind always signified a satisfactory sense of 'case closed' on a meal. A simple jelly can provide such closure – these lovely wobbly forms with their bright colours providing glimpses back to childhood. Greengage was Mma Ramotswe's favourite and when mixed with Ideal milk produces a beautiful colour. She is also particularly partial to Guava. Botswana has an abundance of fresh fruit and Mma Potokwani keeps an eye on the tree in the Orphan Farm, knowing that her husband is partial to a good mango.

Jelly

Ingredients:

A 12 oz tin of evaporated Ideal Milk

Two 5 oz packets of jelly (your choice of flavour)

A tin of crushed guava (optional)

Method:

Keep one tin of Ideal Milk in the fridge overnight. Follow the instructions on the jelly packet but add a little less water. Whip the evaporated milk until slightly thick and add to the jelly just before it sets. Sometimes Mma Ramotswe likes to add a tin of crushed guava for additional flavour and interest.

Light Golden Syrup Cakes

Phuti Radiphuti's Aunt, renowned for her sharp mind and elephant-like memory, clearly remembers what a large tin of golden syrup cost in the late 1950s and wishes she had built up her reserves, being almost down to her last tin. Around payday, Mma Ramotswe had observed the shops filling up with people buying syrup (and beans), a time when she avoided the shops as they increased the prices. However, it was Phuti Radiphuti's Aunt who spotted that this recipe, which had been passed on to her as Gingerbread, did not actually contain any ginger. The cinnamon may lead some who eat your cake to insist that you have added ginger, but most comment on the lightness. Eh, Mma.

Ingredients:

3 tbs margarine

½ cup golden syrup

1 egg

½ tsp salt

1½ cups flour

1 tsp cinnamon

1 tsp bicarbonate of soda

½ cup water

Method:

Cream the margarine. Add the beaten egg. Combine the warmed golden syrup with the water and add alternately with the sifted dry ingredients. Turn at once into a well greased shallow pan. Bake for 30 – 40 minutes (depending on the depth of the batter) at 190°C. Serve warm, with custard as a dessert or cold as a cake.

*. . . the conversation shifted to talk about the first time that either of them remembered eating ice-cream. '
I was eight,' said Mma Ramotswe. 'My father took me to Gaborone and he bought me an ice-cream.
I have never been so excited, Mma. It was a very great day for me.'*

*She closed her eyes. She was standing next to her father, the late Obed Ramotswe, that great man, and he
was handing her an ice-cream. He was wearing his hat, his battered old hat that he wore until the day he
went to hospital for the last time. And he smiled at her from underneath the brim of that old hat, and the
sun was behind him, high in the sky, and the ice-cream tasted sweeter and purer than anything else she
had ever tasted in her life. She would give anything – anything – to have her father back with her, just for
a day, so that she could tell him about how her life had been and how she owed everything to him and to his
goodness to her. It would not take long to tell him all that – about the same length of time it takes to eat an
ice-cream or to walk the length of Zebra Drive. Not long.* (The Miracle at Speedy Motors)

Morula Meringue Pie

Serves 8

Ingredients:

7 oz all-purpose flour	**Pinch of salt**
4 oz shortening	**¼ cup cold water**

For the filling:

11 oz sugar	**1 oz cornstarch**
1 oz all-purpose flour	**Pinch of salt**
1½ cups water	**3 egg yolks, beaten**
1½ oz butter or margarine	**¼ cup *morula* juice**
2 tsp *morula* peel, grated	**1 tsp vanilla essence**

For the meringue:

3 egg whites
1 tsp cream of tartar
3 oz caster sugar

Method:

In a bowl, combine flour and salt; cut in shortening until crumbly. Gradually add water, tossing with a
fork until a ball forms. Roll out pastry to fit a 9 inch pie plate. Transfer pastry to plate. Trim pastry to half
an inch beyond edge of plate; flute edges. Prick bottom and sides of pastry with a fork. Line with a double
thickness of heavy-duty foil. Bake at 230°C for 8 minutes. Remove foil; bake 5 – 6 minutes longer or until
light golden brown. Reduce heat to 175°C.

For filling, combine sugar, cornstarch, flour and salt in a saucepan. Gradually stir in water. Cook and stir
over medium heat until thickened and bubbly, about 2 minutes. Reduce the heat; cook and stir 2 minutes
longer. Remove from the heat. Gradually stir 1 cup hot filling into egg yolks; return all to pan. Bring to a
gentle boil; cook and stir for 2 minutes. Remove from the heat. Stir in butter, *morula* juice, peel and essence
until butter is melted. Cover; set aside and keep hot.

For meringue, whip egg whites and cream of tartar in a mixing bowl on medium until foamy.
Gradually beat in sugar, 1 tbs at a time, on high until stiff glossy peaks form and sugar is dissolved. Pour
hot filling into crust. Spread meringue evenly over filling, sealing edges to crust. Bake at 350°C for 15
minutes or until meringue is golden brown. Cool on a wire rack for 1 hour; refrigerate for at least 3 hours.
Store in the refrigerator.

Rich Chocolate Mousse
Serves 4

Ingredients:

9 oz dark chocolate (traditionally built ladies buy as good as they can get their hands on)
4 oz butter or margarine
5 large free range eggs

Method:

Melt the butter and chocolate in a double-boiler or bain-marie. Take care to avoid the boiling water spilling into the chocolate as it does not do to dilute chocolate. Meanwhile, separate the egg yolks from the whites. When the chocolate and the butter have melted to a thick, smooth mixture, remove the bowl from the saucepan and stir in the yolks, one at a time. In a separate bowl, whip the egg whites until they are stiff and then fold them into the mixture very carefully and tenderly. Don't be alarmed at the quantity of egg white – hold your nerve, this will make a deliciously rich mousse, particularly if you didn't skimp on the quality of the chocolate. Pour the mousse into one family-sized serving bowl or into 4 dessert bowls. Keep in refrigerator 4 hours or longer. Serve with whipped cream. Decorate with glacé cherries (optional for colour).

Banana Fritters

Serves 4

This is a quick, simple dish and doesn't make much mess which your kitchen helper (who may be you) will appreciate. If you are stricken with momentary conscience about the browning state of bananas in your house this is a source of sweet absolution. It is ideal for a snack to tide you through a rainy afternoon, as dessert or even enjoyed for breakfast, going so well with tea.

Ingredients:

Margarine
Half a cup milk
1 tsp vanilla essence (optional)
3 tsps baking powder
Golden syrup

1 cup flour
1 egg
Small pinch salt
3 – 4 bananas cut into halves lengthways
Water

Method:

Sift the flour, salt and baking powder into a bowl. Make a well in centre and break in the egg. Mix and beat well, adding the milk a little at a time. If you wish to, add the vanilla essence. Beat together thoroughly. Dip the pieces of fruit into this batter, one by one, turning each over so that it is well coated. Drop the pieces of batter-covered banana into the hot fat and fry until browned underneath. Turn to brown the other side. Drain well on kitchen paper and serve hot, sprinkled with sugar, maple syrup or chocolate sauce.

Pumpkin Fritters *Serves 4*

Ingredients:

1 cup cooked, drained pumpkin, mashed
Small pinch salt
¾ cup flour
Butter, margarine or sunflower oil for frying

1 egg
1 tbs sugar
3 tsp baking powder
½ tsp mixed spice

Method:

Mix the mashed pumpkin, sugar, salt and mixed spice in a bowl. Break in the egg and beat well together. Stir in the flour and lastly the baking powder, mixing very well. Add a little more flour if needed to make a fairly stiff batter. Melt 2 or 3 tablespoons of fat in a frying pan, and drop the mixture by tablespoonful into the hot fat. Cook until the fritter rises and is brown on the bottom, then slip a knife under it and turn over quickly to brown the other side. Drain on crumpled paper and sprinkle with a little more sugar for serving.

Guava Cake

Ingredients:

2 cups flour

3 tsps baking powder

¼ tsp bicarbonate of soda

½ tsp salt

¾ cup margarine

¾ cup sugar

2 eggs

1 tsp vanilla essence

1 tsp grated lemon rind

1 cup cooked, sieved guava pulp (or drained guava from a tin)

Method:

Sift together three times the flour, baking powder, bicarbonate of soda and the salt. Cream margarine and gradually beat in the sugar until white and fluffy. Add eggs, one at a time, beating well after each addition. Stir in vanilla essence and lemon rind. Add sifted dry ingredients to creamed mixture alternately with guava pulp. Turn batter into 2 greased 8-inch sandwich cake tins and spread evenly. Bake for 30 minutes at 190°C.

Guava Icing

Ingredients:

½ cup butter

2 cups icing sugar

¼ cup guava pulp (or equivalent tinned guava, drained)

a few drops cochineal (if available)

Method:

Cream butter and gradually beat in half the icing sugar. Add the guava pulp and beat in remaining icing sugar. Add cochineal to make a pretty pink colour.

Note: Approximately 1 lb fresh guavas stewed in 1 cup water with ¼ cup sugar and then sieved will make about 2 cups guava pulp.

Green Pawpaw Pudding

. . . shortly after inspecting the pawpaw trees that marked the boundary between her plot and the small piece of wasteland than ran behind it. She had planted the trees herself when first she had come to Zebra Drive and the garden had been nothing, just hard earth, scrub and sour weeds. Now the trees were laden with fruit, heavy yellow orbs that she would shortly pick and enjoy. She liked pawpaw, but neither Mr J.L.B. nor the children did, and so these would be for her alone, a private treat, served with orange juice and topped, perhaps, with a small sprinkling of sugar. (The Miracle at Speedy Motors)

Mma Ramotswe's liking of pumpkin is well known, but perhaps less so is her taste for pawpaw, for which she had cut back the Bougainvillaea, which could rather take over, given the chance. Mma Ramotswe likes pawpaw (which she and Mma Makutsi agreed were loyal, as with other tenacious native vegetation) without much embellishment, but also served with custard or cream according to the following recipe:

Ingredients:

3 tbs self-raising flour	1 tsp baking powder
2 tbs sugar	1 tbs margarine
1 tbs oil	1 egg beaten until it is thick
½ cup milk	lemon rind, ground cinnamon

Green Pawpaw Filling:

Ingredients:

1 medium-sized green pawpaw	Juice of 1 lemon and small piece of peel
Sugar to taste	A few cloves and a little stick cinnamon (optional)

Method:

First make the pawpaw filling. Peel and cut pawpaw into small pieces and boil with the cloves and stick of cinnamon (if used) and a small piece of lemon peel until soft enough to break with a fork, but not soft enough to be mashed. Remove remaining water, break pawpaw with a fork and add the lemon juice first, then the sugar to taste and let it simmer for a while. Keep pawpaw in a cool place and use as required. It freezes well.

Beat sugar, margarine and oil. Add beaten egg little by little, then flour and baking powder, mixing alternately with milk and lemon rind. Cover base of a pie dish with Green Pawpaw Filling and sprinkle with cinnamon and a few pieces of margarine or butter. Cover filling with the cake mixture and sprinkle with a little cinnamon, sugar and a few small pieces of margarine or butter. Bake at 175ºC for 20 minutes or until firm and nicely browned. Serve with fresh cream or custard.

Pawpaw

Rich in vitamins and high in fibre, the Pawpaw or Papaya, as it is known in the United Kingdom and South America, is a highly nutritious fruit. With a light aroma it is deliciously sweet when the ripe fruit is eaten raw, its dark round seeds having been removed. Pawpaw is ripe when it yields a little when squeezed (as with avocados) and its immature green colour has changed to a beautiful orangey yellow. In the UK, we often find the Brazilian variety in supermarkets but the African Pawpaw is larger. Containing the enzyme papain, Pawpaw aids digestion and is an excellent snack or juice that can be enjoyed between meals and which helps counter the blight of constipation. It is also used on minor cuts and abrasions to encourage healing. The plant, that is technically a herb, reaches heights of up to 30 feet with its elongated melon-shaped fruits clustered around the top of a single stem beneath an umbrella of leaves.

Steamed Fig Pudding

Serves 8

Ingredients:

2 oz butter/margarine

4½ oz caster sugar

1 egg

7 fl oz milk

10 oz plain flour, plus 1dsp

4 tsp baking powder

½ tsp vanilla, lemon essence or zest of lemon

9 oz figs (fresh)

Pinch of salt

Method:

Cream margarine or butter and sugar and add beaten egg.

Add milk and mix well.

Add flour, sifted with baking powder and a pinch of salt.

Add essence/zest together with figs chopped into small cubes and throw in one extra dessert spoon of plain flour. Pour into a greased mould. Steam pudding in a saucepan with a lid in 1½ inches of boiling water, for 2 hours, but keep an eye on this and top up to avoid boiling dry.

This is very good served warm with custard, lemon sauce or ice cream.

Lemon Sauce:

boil together ½ cup water and the grated rind of ½ a lemon.
Mix together 2 tbs sugar, 2 tsp corn flour and the juice of ½ a lemon.

Pour a little boiling water over this mixture (enough to cover the base of a small pan), stirring until well mixed.

Put all to saucepan and cook until thick, stirring all the time.

Remove from the heat, add a knob of butter or margarine and stir until melted.

A Last Cup of Tea and Mochudi

. . . if she had any plans for him it was that they would continue to live together in the house on Zebra Drive, that they would grow old in one another's company, and maybe one day go back to Mochudi and sit in the sun there, watching other people do things, but doing nothing themselves . . .

(The Good Husband of Zebra Drive)

As the evening began to take on the colours of the redbush tea that Mma Ramotswe nursed, her thoughts would often turn to Mochudi and to a happy end. She and Mr J.L.B. Matekoni practised their belief in honest effort and hard work, but they looked forward to a time when they would feel content to watch the world go by, carefree and divested of responsibility. The pace of life today called for resilience, self-preservation and some form of sanctuary. For many Batswana, this place of escape was the cattle post. Its pastoral sounds lulled and soothed and the presence and needs of great gentle beasts quelled anxiety. Livestock are an asset and a pension. After work and at weekends, suits, overalls or whatever day-dress disguised the Motswana's true passions would be shed for simple country clothes. Used to sardine-comfort of long bus-journeys and daily commutes on foot for which people elsewhere might seek sponsorship, distance is no barrier to Africans, but when a trip into the bush isn't possible, imagination will transport them there.

Mma Potokwani drew a deep breath. 'I am always happy when I am in the bush,' she said. 'I think everybody is.'

'I certainly am,' said Mma Ramotswe. 'I live in a town, but I do not think my heart lives there.'

'Our stomachs live in towns,' said Mma Potokwani, patting the front of her dress. 'That is where the work is. Our stomachs know that. But our hearts are usually somewhere else.' (The Good Husband of Zebra Drive)

With an encouraging whistle from the stove top, Mma Ramotswe had opened her eyes and examined the residue of tea leaves in the base of her cup as a Go-Away bird dipped overhead, clocking-off. The sun would soon take its rest, but enough light remained and this thinking time and stillness were precious. Another cup of bush tea was fully justified; the perfect evening drink, known to settle worries and which didn't keep her awake. As with the sifting process of sleep, sitting there on the veranda in Zebra Drive, her roaming thoughts often returned not with the quarry, but with clues to its path and a direction that normally encouraged Mma Ramotswe to follow her nose. Small meditative sips and a reverie about the stoep in Mochudi, a vision which she felt sure Mr J.L.B. Matekoni shared. Mma Ramotswe had a pot of redbush tea in Africa, at the foot of Kgale Hill.

Although he was a mechanic, like most people in Botswana he was, at heart, a farmer, and he took great pleasure in his small patch of vegetables that he coaxed out of the dry soil. One day, when he retired, they would move out to a village, perhaps to Mochudi, and find land to plough and cattle to tend. Then at last there would be time to sit outside on the stoep with Mma Ramotswe and watch the life of the village unfold before them. That would be a good way of spending such days as remained to one; in peace, happy among the people and cattle of home. It would be good to die among one's cattle, he thought; with their sweet breath on one's face and their dark, gentle eyes watching right up to the end of one's journey, right up to the edge of the river. (Blue Shoes and Happiness)

Tsamaya sentlě

Acknowledgements

Like his books, Alexander McCall Smith is full of warmth, thoughtfulness and witty encouragement. He has been enthusiastic about this project 'from pumpkin purchase to pudding' and I do appreciate his having faith in me to investigate his characters' culinary passions and to reproduce extensively throughout this book his writing from The No. 1 Ladies' Detective series. My thanks also to Lesley Winton for remembering early cookbook conversations and always being such a pleasure to have contact with. I'm grateful to Neville Moir for wanting to publish this book and his confidence in the format that with a poker player's nerve he has allowed me to evolve and has also guided. Jan Rutherford's energy, positivity and professionalism have been a tonic. A long-time admirer of Iain McIntosh's work, I am delighted that he has continued his relationship with Mma Ramotswe in this book. The brilliant graphic designer Emma Quinn has, as ever, been a delight to work, barbecue and bonfire with: a true artist.

It has been a great pleasure to be part of a team in Botswana with Mats Ögren Wanger, Ulf Nermark and Ulrika Egner. As well as taking beautiful photographs, having produced a very fine documentary together with his wife Cecilia and colleague Ulrika Egner, on the world of Mma Ramotswe, Mats has been a font of ideas. Ulf Nermark too produced these lovely photographs and has been a thoughtful, knowledgeable host and an ethical advocate for all we had contact with, which I admire. Ulrika is a tremendous, energetic fixer who helped make everything happen for us and who is as positive and effective as her Swedish pea soup and schnapps are delicious.

Thank you to the Ministry of Labour and Home Affairs of the Republic of Botswana. The Botswana Council of Women kindly allowed me to reproduce and adapt recipes from *Cooking in Botswana* and I wish them well in reissuing their book. Thanks to Mma Sethokgo Sechele who is understandably much loved and respected by all who know her. Mma Sechele's guidance has been a huge help. Particular thanks also to Amos Mibenge and Grant Read for generously sharing their culinary expertise and recipes and to Frank Taylor of Wildfoods for the wealth of knowledge he imparted about wild fruits. Thanks to Bishop Trevor Mwamba and family for their kind support and assistance and to Sheila Tlou for bringing her style and enthusiasm to this endeavour. I also much appreciate Neil Whitson's help and that of his colleagues at Mokolodi Game Reserve. There are so many people in Botswana and Scotland that have helped through moral support, providing recipes, tasting and trialling.

Thank you to:

Alastair Orford
Alison Anderson
All at GALVmed (the Global Alliance for Livestock Veterinary Medicine)
Alwyn Petersen, Planet Boabab
Andy Quinn
Angela Court-Jackson
Angelica Orford
Anna Herriman & Santi Nieva
Avril Davidson
Baby Molwantwa
Benjie Egner
Bikie Phillip Morebodi
Boithatelo Selabi
Botlhoko Tshosa
Borakanelo Rest, Mochudi
Carol Purcell & Gaud Pouliquen
Caroline & Ged Convey
Catja Orford
Cecilia Wanger
Charles Sheldon
Christel Baudere
Christine Brown
Cowgate Under 5s Nursery
Derek James, S.O.S Village
Dolly & David Grimmer, Lewis and Laura
Dorothy Dambe
Emma Faragher
Everyone at Birlinn Polygon
Fiona & Howard Moffat
Francis Kudumo , Wilderness Safari
Frank & Margaret Taylor and all at Wild Foods
Fungai Makani, Cresta President Hotel
Fuzlin Egner
Göran Hansson, Mapula Lodge
Grace Setlhare
Greta Steele
Hameed Nuru
Helen and Mike Forrester
Jane Garven

Janet Motshoge BCW
Jennifer January Sandstöm
Jenny Egner
Jenny Liddell
Joel Smythe
Josephine Molefe
Judy Moir
Kago E. Modimakwane
Keitumetse Kebonyekgomo
Keleganetse Kealetswe
Kemisoto Nkaelang, Planet Boabab
Kingsley Tlhagwane
Lee Ritchie
Lian Higgins
Luxchman Devtani, The Gaborone Sun Hotel
Lynn McNair
Malakatlou Seitlotleng Ramabele
Malebogo Rakhabi
Malika Faure
Maliki Tapa
Marea Molelekeng
Marie Heyes
Mark Crossan & James Ley
Mary Letsholo
Mmankudu Glickman
Mokolodi Game Reserve
Morwadi Masa, The Gaborone Sun Hotel
Morven Chisholm
Mrs Kopong and aunt, Borakanelo Rest, Mochudi
Ms Agnes Mothobi
Neil Whitson, Mokolodi Game Reserve
Neo Tlhagwane
Nicola Wood
Norman Brown
Onkokame Malope
Ollie Groth, Botswanacraft Marketing
Oshadi Kgafela
Palesa Charissa Motswagole
Patricia Hannah & Colin MacLeod

Patricia Welch
Patrick Chivese, Cresta President Hotel
Pinkie Moloi
Ralph Bousfield, Uncharted Africa
Richard White
Ruth Rowland
Scott Rintoul and Roy Biddle
Sheila Tlou
Sithabile Mathe
Stayce Kenkgetswe, The Gaborone Sun Hotel
Stefan Stjerna
Sue Walker
Susan, the Anglican Diocese, Gaborone
Thato Brian Sebowe
Thato Gaanakgang
The annual Letlhafula
The Cresta President Hotel
The Gaborone Sun Hotel
The ladies of Bahurutshe Cultural Lodge, Mmankgodi Village
The Ministry of Health, Botswana
The No. 1 Ladies' Opera House
The Redbush Tea Company
The Royal Society of Edinburgh
The Rt Rev Bishop Musonda Trevor Selwyn Mwamba
The Staff & Children (particularly House No. 11) of S.O.S Village, Tlokweng
The Staff of the Gaborone Sun Hotel
The Tourism Office next to the President Hotel
Theresa January
Tshepiso Mphele
Unani Matshoga, The Gaborone Sun Hotel
Victoria Dipuo Massey

Most of all, thanks to Kenris and Celeste who accept and adjust to my African comings and goings. Kenris' confidence in and patience with me has been invaluable.

Index

Mma Makutsi is an ardent advocate of the importance of filing systems, of which there are "two main systems. Date or person" (*Blue Shoes and Happiness*). This index adopts the third system, which can of course be easily forgotten, even momentarily by Mma Makutsi, that of subject-matter.

| Traditional baskets and *diphafana*: drinking vessels

Glossary

Baobab, mighty tree and distinctive landmark that grows to incredible circumference and age

Batswana, people of Botswana (plural)

Biltong, cured meat, popular all over Southern Africa

Bogobe, sorghum porridge eaten for lunch/dinner with relish, as a meal in itself or as accompaniment

Botho, observance of manners; proper respect and right way of doing things in Botswana

Braai, (Afrikaans), barbecue

Duiker (Afrikaans), small antelope

Falkirks, see *Pitsana e Maoto a mararo*

Fat cakes, popular traditional pastry

Futswela mollo, blowing on a fire to bring it on

Gaborone, capital of Botswana

Gemere, ginger beer

Go besa mmidi, braising maize cobs in embers of fire

Go fefere, winnowing

Kgotla, public gathering and village court, presided over by the Chief where everyone has a voice

Ko Ko, the correct way in Setswana to announce your presence, whereupon you wait to be invited in

Kika, heavy wooden knee-high mortar

Kolobetsa mabele, steeping process to soften sorghum

Lefetlho, whisk

Lekatane, local variety of melon particularly used for cooking and jam-making (see also *lerotse*)

Lelwapa, circular stone area in village for grain threshing and food preparation

Lerotse, another name for *lekatane*, local variety of melon particularly used for cooking and jam-making

Letsthotlho, cooked, then dried maize kernels

Loselo, shallow basket used for winnowing

Mabele, sorghum

Madila, sour milk

Marie biscuit, a brand of local biscuits, similar to British 'Rich Tea' biscuits

Morula, fruit with nut that grows in abundance; used in jams and snacks

Mealie, maize or corn cob

Mealie meal, maize meal, made from ground maize kernels

Mealie rice, cracked maize kernels, dehulled and pounded to fine granules

Mma, polite form of address to a lady

Mochudi, village from which Mma Ramotswe originates

Mopane worms, caterpillars which are fried as a snack or in stew – a traditional delicacy

Morogo, spinach and other dark leafy vegetables

Mosoko, sorghum or maize meal porridge eaten for lunch/dinner that is a thicker form of *motogo*

Mosukudu, wild mint plant/tea

Mosukujane, wild mint plant/tea

Motogo, soft sorghum or maize meal porridge eaten for breakfast

Motlopi roots, evergreen tree roots that can be fermented and pounded into a coffee-substitute powder

Motshe, large wooden pestle

Motswana, person from Botswana (singular)

Pap, South African term for mealie meal

Peri-Peri, African birdseye chilli

Phaletshe – mealie meal, known by other names elsewhere, including *pap, sadza, ugali*; eaten for lunch/dinner as a meal in itself with relish or as an accompaniment

Phane, Mopane worms

Phate, cow, goat, sheepskin mat used in food preparation

Pitsana e Maoto a mararo (also known as Falkirks), three-legged cauldron-like cooking pot for open fire cooking and gatherings

Pula, currency in Botswana and word for rain

Pawpaw, papaya

Rra, polite form of address to a man

Rooibos (Afrikaans), redbush shrub/tea

Rothwe, wild spinach

Samp, cracked maize kernels, dehulled. Similar to hominy

Serobe, offal

Seswaa, a Botswana speciality, made from pounded/shredded meat, beef or game

Setswana, language and culture of Botswana; pertaining to Botswana

Stoep (Afrikaans), veranda

Thepe, wild spinach

Ting, sour porridge

Tsamaya sentlè, farewell in Setswana, meaning 'go well'